The Predatory Animal Ball

D0963454

The Predatory Animal Ball

Stories

Jennifer Fliss

Okay Donkey Press

© 2021 Jennifer Fliss

All rights reserved.

Printed in the United States of America.

Published by Okay Donkey Press

Los Angeles, CA 90034

www.okaydonkeymag.com

No part of this book may be used or reproduced in any manner without express written permission from the publisher except in the context of articles or reviews.

First Edition. December 2021.

ISBN: 978-1-7332441-6-9

Cover Design: Jennifer Fliss

For G
and for the original G,
my grandma Gloria, z"l

Table of Contents

Pigeons

I once saw a pigeon on Third Avenue hobbling around with a needle sticking out of its eye. Not a small needle either, a long one, about four inches. It swayed like a lightning rod in the wind as the pigeon bobbed its head, talking in its pigeon language. Its I wish I was a dove language. The wrong color language. The wrong place at the wrong time language. The thing is, it didn't look too bothered by the needle. His pigeon friends didn't care. They pecked at crumbs and street debris. It tottered on brittle orange feet.

Watercolor Felon

I awaken to a blossom of blood. Petals of crimson slowly water-coloring outward. See how it grows? It'd be beautiful if it wasn't so fucking tragic. He says, *why'd you have that beer? I told you* – And I stop him right there with the eyes and the hands of a killer. I say he'd better not, and then a tsunami heaves up and out comes all the debris – splintered house and broken bones. Eventually we sleep in different rooms and love the walls the way we once loved each other. He only looks at me through his peripheral vision. Never straight on. I also only look at his shadows. It's like there's a warrant out for me and my crimes, but everyone is too scared to approach, like I'm a junkyard dog. So they leave me scraps that I must pilfer on my own. I'm an artist now. Poor, starving artist.

Sex Drive

The fine people who live on Sex Drive are often seen as a wanton lot. The road ends in a cul-de-sac, where whispers and gossip collect, in front of 1960 modern – not so modern anymore – houses.

They should not be blamed for taking advantage of a real estate market that allowed them to purchase a small lot with a large house, much larger than their needs. They would not have been able to get into this neighborhood otherwise.

One thing to note: her sex drive is not the same as his sex drive. She sees oaks and maples and the peeling paint of the house across the street. He sees that the wife across the street mows the lawn in very short shorts and that their lawn is very close cut.

The mailman, the milkman, the gas company reps; they stop into Sex Drive and they leave behind eyes, behind curtains, behind perfectly clean windows. Peekaboo to the children and to each other. The curtains a heavy damask with a trail of gold swirling through the fabric. Lacquered nails trace the pattern, if not bitten to the quick.

A tired worn block in a tired worn suburb outside a tired worn city under a halcyon sky.

After a big rain, the gutters are useless. The puddles become ponds, become small lakes. You might consider them water features. If you look closely enough, you can see up the neighbor's skirt, as she brazenly tromps through the iridescent, oily water. But you don't have to do that, since you can see up her skirt any old time. That's the thing when you live here.

Oh! The townspeople laugh, a glint of jealousy in their eyes, you live on Sex Drive, do you? Wink, wink. Nudge, nudge. Except that last one was not a nudge, but a pat on your thigh, no not a pat, but a rub, a caress. Is it wanted? Is it wonted?

They come to parties, to dinners, and they leave a little less sure of their own place on Evergreen Lane and Willow Creek Trail.

The fine folks of Sex Drive have created a neighborhood watch. They watch, they listen, they salivate at the thought of being watched and listened to. So do you, don't you?

Dandelions

You pick dandelions. Haven't done the yard in months, so there are hundreds of the little infectious yellow bursts carpeting what you dare to call a lawn. Someone said once, or you read, you think, that dandelions can help you sleep. Under your pillow or crushed up and sprinkled on your sheets. Or something like that. And you haven't slept in weeks, so you stand in your bare feet in the dewy wet overgrowth and bend to pick the flowers. Weeds – no, flowers.

After the boys are asleep – they are thirteen and seventeen so not really boys anymore – you stand under the single, naked lightbulb in the bathroom. You watch the fluorescent of the metal wiring inside as it flickers. You marvel at how much science is in these household things. Think about how these round bulbs are being replaced by those modern Guggenheim Museum bulbs with their infinite curves and promises to live on and on and on. Tucked into your Bible, which you haven't opened in years, is a postcard from the New York museum. On the back it just reads *Art as Fuck,*

Bob. You're not sure why you keep it, the postcard or the Bible. Anyway, you often have to use the toilet in the dark because of the crappy light. The landlord won't do shit. That's what he says. *I won't do shit. You don't pay me enough for shit.*

You spread moisturizer on your parchment skin – also you can't turn the heat off and it's June. The cream feels like its coagulated blood. You assume, anyway.

You gather the dandelions from the dresser and pull off the flowers, dropping the stems and their forked leaves to the floor. Scrunch up the soft yellow flowers in your fist to smell the pungent herby scent.

You remember making headbands out of dandelions as a child. You wanted to find the ones with the longest stems. Some people drink dandelion tea. Eat the greens. Dandelion wine. What kind of horrible thing is that? Bitter, you assume these people are bitter.

You pull back your blanket, exposing the bare mattress, silvery flowers with stitched curves. Drop the petals slowly. The pulpy remnants and stems you slide under the pillow. Your ex-husband used to stash his handgun under your head, and you'd fall asleep with an oily hunk of metal pushing into your ear. He would slip his thick hand under that same pillow when he came to bed. It was a gesture that, if you didn't know what his hand was clutching, you'd think was romantic.

Your oldest calls out. He does that in his sleep. You check the door to the boys' room. It's still shut. Your oldest also gets up in the middle of the night, drinks milk from the carton and leaves the fridge open. He does that in his sleep too.

A shotgun rings. Or a car backfires. Mid-step, you startle, then freeze, refusing even to place the heel of your foot down. Wait to hear something more. Wait to hear from your boys. Nothing. They've slept through it. You open their door, just a crack, listen to the teenage snoring; warbling love, slobber, and exhaust.

A blue nightlight shines on your youngest, making him appear underwater. You want to yank the light from the wall, but you know if he wakes up without it, in the dark, he'll scream something ghastly and wet the bed. Leave it. The image stays with you, your drowning son.

Back in bed with the crumbled weeds; the forgotten flower that you loved so much but now just stinks like shit and derelict houses. You brush them from the mattress, but some get ground in. Try to pick each petal out, but your nails are bitten to the quick and they can't get purchase against the soft mattress.

From under your pillow, you brush what you can of the dandelions onto the floor. With broad strokes you desperately try to get it all. You finally lay under the blanket, hot but needing the weight on you. You hear the fridge open and fall asleep listening to the glug of milk and the smell of earth beneath you and in your fingers and on your palms.

You sleep the whole night through, and in the morning, you drift through the weedy debris of the night on your way to the kitchen. You think about vacuuming, but remember the vacuum is broken. Has been all year. You'll need to pick out the plant bits from the grubby carpet with your fingers. You'll have to let your fingernails grow for that.

Pretty soon the flowers in the yard will turn puffy and white, and with each wish, blow off in the wind and no one will know they were there in the first place, crowding your lawn, helping you sleep, protecting you.

Degrees

63 degrees: It is spring. We are languishing on the hoods of our cars in the school parking lot, that's otherwise empty because it's a Saturday. A Chrysler from the 80s, a Ford truck from the 70s, a Lexus from 1998, a newer model Corolla, and a shiny new Tesla. If it were October and this temperature, we'd already be wearing jackets. But it's early spring, and the weeds are pushing up and we are all heady from the winter hibernation.

72 degrees: We discuss going to the swimming hole, which is really just a lake that has been strangled by condo developments until it became a meager reflection of its former self. We discuss it, but we don't actually go. There's still a bite in the air when we're wearing nothing.

77 degrees: We go to the swimming hole. We wear over-sized vintage tee shirts advertising bands we've never listened to. The water is still chilly. The rocks beneath our bare feet are slimy

and soft, and we clench our toes to keep us steady. We take water into our mouths and spit it upward like we are cupid statues. The water tastes like jasmine and gasoline and it coats our hair, and in our wannabe-hippie way, we insist it cleanses our souls.

84 degrees: We are up early. We don't wear shoes while we run around the grass and balance on a slack line we've tied between two trees. We have picnics and sweat slips down our backs when we chase after girls we are crushing on.

87 degrees: We fall into bushes and beds and sandy beaches and make out. Our adolescent glistening sweat tells us we are doing it right. This is passion, we think. It's what we've been told to believe. We believe it.

99 degrees: We have grown lazier. We stay in bed with the sheets pushed to the floor. The power has gone out again, so the a/c isn't working. We say we'll meet up, but we bail. We stay home, lethargic under the tent of a book and on chairs that rock slowly, or we doze on porches as insects bite at our skin.

102 degrees: *Christ, it's hot*, we say over and over and over again. We fan ourselves with pieces of paper: takeout menus, homework, Japanese paper fans we saved from a samurai-themed party we threw last summer. We take to our cars and drive fast with the windows down to feel the sandy air on our faces.

106 degrees: We grow irritable. The meteorologists can't explain the heat wave. It's hotter in D.C., they say. At least there's that.

110 degrees: On TV, the politicians' ties are loosened. As soon as they're out of the building, their jackets are off too. It makes for a much more casual government. Climate change has finally hit the Republicans, people on social media chirp.

114 degrees: Sandstorms pick up debris of our lifetime. Takeout bags from the burger place. Receipts. Crumpled grocery lists. Post-its and classifieds ads. Children's sandboxes empty. Gardens lift on the air leaving naked seeds. The birds pick at these hopefully. The phantom wind whips around the corners of our houses surprising us, even though we've been hearing it for weeks. The ghost runs his devilish fingers along the siding, letting us know he's just outside.

117 degrees: Our crimson skin erupts into tiny Mount Vesuviuses.

125 degrees: The plants frizzle and char like roasted vegetables left out too long, which indeed they are. Our air conditioning fails. Our electricity fails. Our water fails. Our crops fail. Our hospitals fail. Our long-term plans fail. Our hope fails. Our relationships fail.

132 degrees: Our short-term plans fail. Our minds fail. Our hearts fail. Our bodies fail.

147 degrees: The sand collects on the leather interior of our vehicles, scratching the CDs left out on passenger seats. They will never be able to play music again. Even if there were equipment to play it on and hands to do it, it would be garbled half-versions of the stories they meant to tell.

150 degrees: First the tires are covered. The wind pushes the sand up more and more until the doors are stuck shut. The sand covers them entirely, leaving metal sarcophagi, to become never visited monuments to commemorate our inventiveness.

162 degrees: We are all dead.

194 degrees: Our vehicles and buildings and the remnants of our hopes begin to melt into silvery solder.

200 degrees: The phantom surveys his kingdom. Finally, silence. The empty desert expanse undulates under its breath. The scorched earth was a map of three-dimensional hieroglyphics depicting the life that was. The phantom rolls up the sand, balls it up, feels the grittiness of it, and drops it down, down, down to the earth, burying bodies – ignored carrion – creating dunes where there were none.

Just the Air That They Breathe

A tiny woman lived in the little terrarium that hung in Mr.
and Mrs. Barker's kitchen window. After her third miscarriage,
Mrs. Barker drove herself to Buck's Nursery and told the salesman
she couldn't keep things alive. Well, an air plant would be a good
start, he told her. They didn't even need soil, just the air that they
breathe. Maybe give them a spritz of water here and there and they
will thrive, he said.

Mrs. Barker bought a spiky *melanocrater*, a thumb-sized
grassy *filifolia*, and a green *tillandsia ionantha* with pink tips. To
house them, she bought a round glass terrarium the size of a fist.
To go with it, she purchased a small bag of perfectly tan sand.

From a dusty make-up bag, Mrs. Barker found tweezers
and an eyeshadow brush and used the utensils to place the plants
just so and arrange the sand. She hung the terrarium in the window
over the kitchen sink so she could see her plants often.

The woman that lived in the terrarium took up residency
about a month in, when the plants' not often talked about fragility

was beginning to show. The tips were browning, and the reedy leaves began to weep.

Mrs. Barker had not invited the mysterious squatter in and didn't even know she was there. The woman in the terrarium was unsure of how she got there herself, but she went about her work anyway. She spoke to the plants in soft whispers. Sotto voce, she said *live*. She lifted their arms when they drooped. She nourished the air around them and they, in turn, took it all in.

One day, while cleaning their two dinner plates free of Salisbury steak, Mrs. Barker heard a faint voice, so faint she thought it must have been her imagination, or something caught in the radiator. It was like a faint waterfall and brought to mind cradles and wispy hair and rocking, and Mrs. Barker began to hum along. Eventually, the hum turned into her voice and she sang, as she finished the dinner dishes. She kept on as she spritzed her little plants. She didn't stop. Lullabies, Simon and Garfunkel, Van Halen, Christmas carols, it didn't matter. She sang while she showered. She sang while she cooked. Did she imagine one of the reeds of the *melanocrater* waving? She kept singing.

A month after that, Mr. Barker remarked upon how well the plants were doing. *They are beautiful*, he said and gave her a *chlorophytum comosum*, a common spider plant. Wiry offshoots from the main plant filled the container and from one shoot came a smaller plant, and another, and still another. They all resembled the main spider. Mrs. Barker later learned they were referred to as

The mother and her spiderettes. She invited the self-propagating creature in.

The woman in the terrarium knew that her work in the terrarium was done. One morning Mrs. Barker placed the spider plant next to the sink. As she filled the watering can, the woman in the terrarium jumped. She immersed herself in the warm loamy soil of the spider plant.

One year later, the woman in the spider plant was gone. Seven baby spiderettes had flourished. Mrs. Barker sang to her numerous plants, and the Barkers' house was filled with a quiet breathing.

The Mourning Light

We had been in our cell for two days before they came to us. We were famished and wondering when-oh-when would we get out. Would we ever escape the time-too-still, gut-heaving, clenching-jaw of this sadness?

There were just the two of us. Food on trays had been brought, but we could not eat. Water too; we took small sips, refusing the quench. What right did we have to work to sustain our lives? Life too adjacent to us had been taken. Not in my back yard, people say. So where then? On your front steps, your porch, your dining room with the chandelier sparkling overhead?

"Turn out the light," I told her.

"Turn off the light," she said.

"What?"

"Turn it off. Not out. You said it wrong."

"People say turn out the light," I said.

"But it's wrong. All the people are wrong," she said. That was true. All the people were wrong.

We were just passing through when our mother was slaughtered by a roving band of criminals. *Oh yes. They are terror,* the people of the village said and bowed their heads. They too lost loved ones. We became citizens of this small, mysterious place. They burned her body, her clothes, a rough effigy. They sobbed while drumming and singing throaty chants, as if it had been their own blood spilled across the grass. My sister and I were ushered into a cabin. Thin mattresses, beautiful patchwork quilts, a mirror covered in gauzy muslin, a glassless window in the door.

Now, after two days, an old woman knocked and entered our small room. She held out her hand to help us stand and then bowed.

"I am very sorry," she said, as she set down another tray of food. Removed the ones collecting flies that we had ignored.

She then handed us a lantern. Primitive, a glass encasement open at the top, a small metal knob, blue-yellow flame. She pointed to a hook in the middle of the circular room.

"Hang it there." We did. "It is the bereavement lantern," she told us. "You can mourn for as long as this light is lit."

"When does it go out?" I asked.

"It is different for everyone," she said.

"Who made them?" I asked.

"I do not know," she said.

"How does it work? I mean, how does it know when we are done?" my sister asked.

"I do not know," she repeated, and left us to the dark and of our sorrowful light. I watched the flame flicker, eating moths in its effervescence.

I ate a small bread roll. My sister still wanted for no food. The yeasty thickness of it brought to mind so many loaves of bread made growing up. Our mother's soft hands were permanently powdered with flour. As she ran her hands through our hair and along our legs, she left behind fine white dustings, like she was already a ghost.

I slept. I slept and I hadn't slept since we found her mangled carnage. Closing my eyes would bring forth her lopped off fingers and begging blue eyes, wet and dark with smeared mascara, the only makeup she wore. This time, when I closed my eyes, I saw a kitchen, gingham tablecloth and matching curtains, rooster-shaped salt and pepper shakers, savory chicken livers, pulpy orange juice. And then I fell asleep.

"What is the difference between bereavement and mourning?" My sister asked the next morning. "And sadness," she added.

"I'm not sure," I said, as I rolled over. I had slept the whole night. Couldn't remember dreaming. "Maybe levels? Like *how* sad."

Or distance?" she asked. She was folding her quilt. Perfect corner to corner. She didn't turn to look at me. Just folded and folded and folded. "Time?"

"Yeah, or that," I agreed.

I mean, you can be sad forever"

"Yes."

"Bereavement seems like sitting *shiva*. Like it's a set period of time," my sister said.

"So you think we will be here for seven days?" I asked.

"No one is keeping us here," my sister motioned to the door. That was true. There was no lock on our cell. No guards. This was not an imprisonment. We had done nothing wrong. My sister kept folding. The square of blanket grew smaller.

"We could go home," I suggested, knowing this would not be suitable for either of us. It was not what our mother would have wanted, and it was not what I wanted.

We didn't leave. Food trays were delivered and each day the trays grew emptier when the old woman came to take them away. The flame kept up. It occasionally grew sparse, with a strong breeze or an unseen force, but it kept burning. We counted dead moths, but lost count at thirty-three. Who would mourn these insects, the less vibrant country cousin to the butterfly? If its wings were more vivid, would we cry for them?

We didn't cry for them. Perhaps we should have. But we emptied ourselves for our mother. The old woman entered once while my sister and I held each other, and sobbed into each other's bodies, filling each other up when the other depleted. Upon the woman's arrival, we both sat up, dabbed at our teary cheeks, sniffled apologies.

"Do not apologize for love," she said, as she placed another tray down. She walked to the lantern, didn't touch it, silently assessing it. She carefully took it down and tipped the moth carcasses into her hand. The flame remained lit.

"These moths have to come to the light, you know? It's part of who they are." We still sat there, trying to make sense of this woman and the dead not-butterflies and the light and our mother who was also a dead not-butterfly.

"I will take these out," the old woman said and crushed them into ash in her fist and dispersed the remains on the floor. That night, when my sister had folded her blanket into the smallest square she could, I approached the lantern. The moths were beginning to collect again. I turned the metal knob. With a violet hiss, the light went out. We emerged from the cell. In the darkness, we carried with us a small torch with which to guide the way home.

Evidence

Exhibit #104

Item: an oversized postcard, size: 8.5 x 5.5

The prosecutor reads its contents aloud.

It was so weird. I was eating the cherry pie – local they said, but it tasted like maraschino – and this guy approaches. Real tall. Forehead you could fry an egg on, maybe two. And an eyebrow – just one – that would never allow sweat to pass his baby doll eyelashes. He looked alien, but familiar. Strange, but beautiful.

He slid right into the booth next to me. Reached over me and grabbed a menu from behind the napkin holder, said he was famished. I just stared at the table, a map with no place names, lines on the linoleum, intersecting and circling around. But I didn't ask what he was doing. I don't know why not.

Then the waitress came around, took his order. Never looked up and left.

The man with the brow pointed his thick but manicured finger at the postcard I was about to write. "Postcards, yeah? Not from around here, yeah? I come here all the time. I get the turkey club. Safe bet." He pointed to the sign that declared the cherry pie best in the county was here in this diner. "Bullshit," he said. "Yeah? Bullshit? Right? My grandmother makes the best and she's just down the road. If you ever wanted to try it." And here he grew a little shy. "Like a date?" I asked. "Yeah, I mean, sure."

"Real cherry pie, that is. None of this Shirley Temple in a frozen piecrust stuff," and then he picked up a bent fork and helped himself to the rest of my pie. Can you believe it?!

"You can leave a trace, if you're worried," he said. "Here, write it down here. And then this way someone knows who you're with. Where you've gone. Write it, here. I've got a stamp. Now, who do we send it to?"

xoxo,
Mae

Infidelity Love Suit

The gabardine is itchy; he wears it like his trimmed beard. He smells of rum and doesn't always wash, and his tongue also smells of rum and sounds like a cat lapping up milk, as it licks the intricate curves of my ear, tracing it like a map he knows and doesn't need.

The infection is now presenting itself as a phone call unanswered. I dial back but get a flower shop. I dial again and get the Chinese restaurant. Antibiotics sometimes have negative side effects; this I know.

His brogues have lost their tread, he may slip at any moment in the slick I've left when I emptied myself onto the floor. But he has kicked off the shoes, and they lay, one upside down, on the eggshell white carpet of our bedroom.

Take it to the dry cleaners, he instructs, while in the shower, steam like ashes on the glass. I collect the things from the toilet seat. Torn cuticles on my hands catch on the fabric, threaten to unravel it all. But I bite them instead. *Don't do that,* he tells me, as if he can see through the glass at the ghost of me.

Again, the phone rings and I answer. *Hello.* I hear her breath. Or his. And the clatter of the elevated train is back there, too and someone is yelling about Jesus. It's not he or she yelling about Jesus, of course. But, just as I'm about to be told what will happen to me in the next coming, when the messiah visits, the line goes dead.

I throw the suit on the passenger seat and, as I back out of the driveway, it slithers to the floor to rest with dried fir needles and tissues. I pull into the dry cleaners, which shares a parking lot with the Chinese restaurant. *24-hour turnaround!* A neon sign shouts. Beside the building is a green dumpster. Taller than me. Smells of sardines and banana peels and rainwater. I reach up and push the suit over the edge. It doesn't make a sound on the other side. A section of sleeve dangles above me, half in, half out. A seagull overhead caws. I get into the car and go home.

You took the suit in? he asks later. I did, I say, and I tell him it'll be ready in 24 hours.

Edward Scissorhands Takes Up Scrapbooking

Edward Scissorhands has taken up scrapbooking. He lives in Amagansett and meets, three times a week, with the six other ladies that form a scrapbook circle. After the city-folk have gone, the group meets at Lorraine's house for tea and sometimes something stronger. This early fall day, the group sits on Lorraine's porch as they measure, cut, paste, and reminisce.

Lorraine admires Edward's dexterity despite the onset of rust. *Aging does that,* says Edward Scissorhands, who has long gotten over childhood speech impediments that hindered him when he was young. Lorraine will often run her own old, wispy hands along Edward's blades. She has been a widow for twenty-three years. Her Jack could julienne a carrot in three seconds flat. He would have liked Edward.

Edward Scissorhands lives in the guest house behind Marjorie's cottage. The cottage has seven bedrooms and five-and-a-half bathrooms. An indoor and outdoor pool. A sauna, which Edward is allowed to use and does – often. Marjorie was the one who invited him into their craft circle. He was grateful. At the time, few people trusted a man with sharp hands. In fact, most probably still don't.

Edward is working on a scrapbook of his recent trip to Europe. He went with several members of the scrapbooking circle, as well as Eleanor Shipley, the librarian. They chartered a bus that took them to seven countries: England, France, Germany, Austria, Italy, Spain, and Andorra.

Edward has collected the following from the trip: twenty-three photos; two boarding passes; two stolen menus; twelve museum tickets; eight postcards; one bookmark; four pressed flowers; a sliver of wood from *their* tree in Paris; a flyer for a lost dog in Lyon; three postage stamps; a five euro note; a seating chart of the Vienna Opera House; on hotel stationery, in Lorraine's sloppy handwriting, a line from a poem she saw on a Parisian wall: *Un bateau frêle comme un papillon de mai;* and two tickets to *Don Giovanni*, one ripped and one unused. Beside that pile, Edward has a shoebox with a selection of stickers, colored pens, tape, ribbon, and an array of card stock.

Look, Big Ben. A selfie taken with a stoic palace guard. Parliament. A group photo on the train to Paris taken by a gracious porter. Statue of Napoleon. Lorraine, amidst a flurry of cherry blossoms in Jardin du Luxembourg. Some monkeys in Granada. Edward alone in the middle of Las Ramblas. Here, a photo of Lorraine and Edward in front of the Eiffel Tower. She is pretend-ing to take a bite out of a baguette. Edward doesn't smile in photos but he was happy. He doesn't really smile much ever, in fact, photo or not.

A run of the glue stick over the back of the photo and onto the page it goes. He presses puffy stickers of bread products onto the page. With his teeth, he removes the cap of a gel pen. In fine cursive he writes, *Ooh La La.*

Edward enjoys scrapbooking. It allows for contemplation of the activities in which he partakes. It's almost like having the experience a second time. As he lays down more puffy *brioches,* he can smell the boulangeries – the yeast, the flour, the early morning pungency of the Seine. Bread is so much more romantic than flowers.

On their last day in Paris, Edward presented Lorraine with a cone of chouquettes, small puffs of airy bread coated in coarse sugar. As she ate, sugar pearls dotted the space between her upper lip and her nose. He motioned to her. *You have a little something...* She couldn't get it all and Edward leaned in to brush it away.

Despite the years of practice, and despite his comfort and the comfort of others, when Edward Scissorhands slips and draws blood, it is always alarming. It is like he becomes a stranger all over again. Lorraine pressed her hand into her lip and ran off to the bathroom.

Edward's heart cleaved with the wound. After that, he sat in the back row of the bus, next to the tiny bathroom. The ladies all said 'hello' when they came to relieve themselves, invited him to come up front, but Edward preferred to keep some distance after the accident.

After Paris, they moved on: Versailles, Normandy, Lyon. Into Italy: Milan, Rome. In a Venetian canal, after he watched Lorraine board a gondola by herself, he stared into the water as his reflection grew murky and the ashy clouds overhead let loose a shout of thunder and explosive tears. Edward too was crying, but the rain covered it all up by the time he returned to the bus.

In his scrapbook, he uses teal tape to attach a ticket from the Doges' Palace. He places the tape at jaunty angles to express that he is lighthearted about that day in Venice when it rained.

In a beer hall in Munich, Edward spilled an entire pitcher on himself and the librarian. He was not drunk, but he feigned a buzz and retreated to his hotel room. It was hours before the ladies returned. He could hear them in the next room shouting *Proust* over and over and over again. It was Lorraine that said, *enough already, you morons. It's prost, not Proust.*

Edward has cut-outs of mini beer steins, which do not have a sticky back, so he has to use glue to stick them onto the next page of his book. This is the delicate work of a scrapbooker; some of the details are so small, so minuscule, that even the finest fingers struggle with placement.

Edward stands. "Just need a break," he says. After sitting for so long and concentrating on such meticulous work, he needs to stretch. The ladies keep their eyes down: snipping, pasting, flipping through photos.

Edward steps off the porch. Kicking up auburn fall leaves, he watches as they settle back into piles. Luxury cars pass by far too fast, too close to the sidewalk. Tires slap into the divots where dirty puddles collect. Edward is careful to step aside when cars draw near. But a Hummer, too wide for the road anyway, sends up a deluge of water. Soaked, Edward curses the driver, shakes out his sleeves, and turns around. He had walked only two blocks, but the tiny heads of the craft circle look impossibly far away.

The women are not gossiping in his absence. They bob and nod their heads to the cadence of their artwork. Only Edward's seat is empty. And, he notices, Lorraine's. Back through the dead-leaf corridor, Edward ascends the rickety stairs. His hair, already lank and weepy, is dripping. His slip-on, black and white checkered sneakers, bought at the insistence of the teenager in the town's only shoe store, saturated. His feet squeak on the deck. He can't risk getting his memorabilia wet. It'd ruin the whole book. The whole story.

But then a towel is around his shoulders. A monogram indecipherable in its script brushes his cheek. Lorraine begins to rub the towel against his shoulder blades.

"That jerk," she whispers into his ear. "He lives over on Georgica. Anyway, can't send you home like that. Come on in. We'll get you into something dry."

Edward Scissorhands never gets further than Munich. Never returns to his teeny, tiny beer steins. The scrapbook ends there.

The Child Executioner

The boy didn't know what the man was in for. Was he a pervert? A murderer? Did people just not get him? Was he all three? The boy only knew that he was a bad man, and he was going to die. He understood about death. In his eight years, he had lost a cat, two rabbits, his grandfather, and a cousin to death. His mother said they'd gone to heaven. The boy thought it seemed wrong that heaven was muddy and cold, and that they had to leave flowers every so often at the gates of heaven. Weren't there flowers there already? Wouldn't they not all die? Isn't that the whole job of heaven?

At the appointed time, *when the big hand is here and the little hand is here*, the boy was to push the button. He had practiced the day before. The button was blue, like that bus he saw with his mother that one time. The button was half-dollar sized and affixed to the wall. There was no sign to indicate what it was the button did. No warning at all, which struck the boy as odd, since the button could be pushed accidentally and awful bad things would happen. But, when he practiced, the boy couldn't press down hard enough. The warden held his potato-fat thumb over his and showed him how to press in the center very hard. *You gotta mean it, son.*

Mom, why is that school bus blue? The boy had asked when he saw the bus stopped at a traffic light. What school were the kids going to? Was Carol also driving that bus? Did people scratch rude drawings and their names into the seats? His mother explained it was filled with filthy and evil people. He wondered what schoolchildren had to do to be considered evil. His mother dragged him across the crosswalk and when he looked up, he saw that it was not Carol in the driver's seat and that bars covered the windows. In the back, the boy thought he saw familiar jagged teeth in a darkened face. His mother pulled him onward.

The bad man shuffled and was shoved along by one of the guards. It seemed like he was scared of what was to come. The boy knew the feeling. Every Sunday night, his father and his girlfriend came for dinner. When the boy was called downstairs from his room and had to kiss his father on the lips, the boy also found that he shuffled like the bad man.

He was tall, like his father, but bald, not like his father, who had red curly hair, sometimes worn in a ponytail. The bad man wore a khaki jumper. It didn't have feet, and his sneakers didn't have laces.

Before he walked out on the boy and his mother, his father gave him a stuffed bear. The boy thought the bear looked sad, so he surveyed his sister's dolls and determined that the perfectly round, cherry cheeks were what made a doll happy. He used bubblegum to create doughy pink blush on the bear. Eventually the gum lost its tackiness, turned gray, and had to be sheared off. The bear was named Gummy and his marred face reminded the boy of the bad man's face, uneven craters and shadowy facial hair. One day, his mother threw Gummy out with the trash. *It was an accident*, she said.

Behind the boy, two guards discussed the bad man's last meal. Peanut butter and jelly on white bread. Pickle. Chocolate milk. *Like his mother would have made,* one of them said. *Asshole,* said the other.

The boy was allergic to peanuts. When he was four, his father and his mother took him out to a seafood restaurant where peanut shells carpeted the floor. When the boy began wheezing before even the water was poured, his father told him to quit his dramatics. When the chowder was delivered, the boy passed out. His mother cradled him, as his father finished his soup, wiped up the rest with his sourdough bread, and then they left with the anaphylactic child.

For his last meal, the boy would have chosen fried chicken, strawberries – fresh, not store bought – potato chips with ridges, waffles, and chocolate milk. Just like the bad man.

The room the boy was in had dials and knobs and buttons covering the wall. Two black-and-white televisions hung in the corners and four women congregated there. Two were guards, on wore a tight, black dress even the boy knew was inappropriate, and the other woman stood behind the boy and gripped his shoulder. When he tried to look at her face, she clawed tighter. He stopped trying to look. Her nails were painted green, and the boy thought how her fingers looked like carrots gone bad, all shriveled left in the crisper drawer too long.

Large windows looked down over the execution room, which looked like a barn, but instead of red walls and animals, it was gray and had twelve people in the room. The boy counted. The bad man was led to a chair in the center of the room. His arms were strapped down, and a priest stood beside him. The boy could see the priest's lips moving.

"I don't want to do it," the boy said.

"You don't have to," the owner of the green claws said.

"I'm not going to do it," he said.

"You don't have to," she repeated, but she didn't remove her hand from his shoulder.

On the wall above the boy, a large digital clock read 00:10 in big, blood-colored numbers. Okay then, said one of the guards. The claw squeezed the boy's shoulder, and in his ear whispered, *Are you ready?* The boy nodded except he was lying. The numbers began to tick downward. 9, 8, 7. The boy looked at his thumb. Push hard, he thought. If you don't… if you don't… he couldn't remember what he had been told. What would happen if he didn't push hard? There had been some sort of warning. His was the most important job, he knew. 5, 4, 3. He flexed his thumb, he bent his thumb – stretching the small muscles. The boy looked down at the bad man, who, he saw had his head turned upward. He looked at the boy and nodded. The clock reached 0 and flashed red.

Towels

The baby is born at home. This isn't planned. In a blizzard in Wisconsin, she slips out of her mother and is wrapped, a slush of vernix and blood. A blue child in a crisp white towel.

We are going to the beach. We carry sunblock and water and snacks. The kids haul pails and shovels. Towels decorated with fish and polka dots and Mickey Mouse flung over our shoulders as we tromp through the sand. We lay them out and position our bodies on them as the surf comes in and goes out, and we watch our children play.

Cotton. Durable. Washable. Imported.

I had too many margaritas. After the searing hot shower, I step out and blanket myself in the towel. I rub my eyes; black slicks of partying and drinking and dancing. Smeared remnants of *Can I buy you a drink?* I consider getting back into the purifying font of the shower. *C'mon... you don't mean that.* I still haven't been able to wash it all away.

She was babysitting the two-year-old. It was her first day and she wanted to get it all right. On a subdivided plate made of environmentally friendly material, she placed cut pears, cheddar squares, thumb-sized carrots. She poured the milk into a matching cup. From upstairs, the child screamed out, a prehistoric yowl that caused the babysitter's hands to slip. Milk glugged onto the counter, pooling at the edge and slipped down to the floor. She bent and mopped it up with a dishtowel, the cloth sucked up the liquid and grew heavy. The baby still cried.

At the very exclusive club at the very end of the boulevard at the very end of the island, the towels were burgundy and white striped. If you had a towel that was not burgundy and white striped, it was clear you did not belong. Lying atop burgundy and white striped towels were CEOs, hedge fund managers, heirs, actors, and trust fund teenagers. After only a handful of washes, the like-new but too-used-for-the-clientele towels found their way into the homes of the housekeepers, pool attendants, reservations staff, and waiters. If they couldn't pay their rent with the eleven-dollar-an-hour wages, they at least felt like they were two steps instead of one, from the street if they folded themselves into the luxurious cotton.

Wash with similar colors. Tumble dry on medium heat. No bleach. Cleaning instructions in home economic hieroglyphics.

You are sitting in the glow of your computer. Scrolling through the hundreds of towels. They look soft. Are they as plush as they look? 100% Egyptian cotton? Turkish? What color? Slate? Ash? What about aubergine? Lilac? Your fiancé said definitely no purple. If they are not called purple, are they purple?

They were robins. The blue of their shells still lined the bottom of the nest. Where was their mother? You understand you shouldn't mess with nature. That you shouldn't touch or feed or nurture in any way, these fine brittle chicks. But they are right by your kitchen window. And you can't help but open the window to hear their earnest chirps. A crow hovers near. Those brilliant, evil harbingers of chaos. You can't bear the thought. You hurry around the house. Towel, syringe from the infant Tylenol, a large shoebox. You line the shoebox with red and green shredded party paper that had been in a gift bag carrying a tiny, embroidered pillow from your mother-in-law. It read *What Part of MEOW don't you understand?* You don't have a cat. You go out to the nest. There are now three crows perched on the gutter. With a hand towel you lift the nest and place it in the box. Careful. Careful. One little robin is particularly vehement, and you name it Stevie, and you nurse the three birds over the next month. The mother robin doesn't return. You release the three birdies into your yard.

There are five crows watching you from the gutter. You watch and you wait, and you only see one robin ever return.

There is a fire. Wet the towel, throw it over your head. Run like hell.

Algodon. Hecho en China.

Harold, the mastiff, rubs his 110-pound body in the mud. Though still large, Harold is underweight, and his owners are discussing – hushed and tearful – euthanasia. The coolness of the earth soothes Harold's worn self while fresh drops of rain tickle his nose. Harold has been waiting for this, the arid summer too long, too difficult for his tremendous, aging body. *Harold! Here boy!* Hauling his body around, he slips and slides through the door into the kitchen, mud slicking the linoleum. A towel is thrown over his thick body, and he is hugged and dried and hugged again.

Natalie surveyed the hotel room. In the middle of the king-sized bed were two origami towel frogs. She had seen swans of this ilk before. But never frogs. Were they trying to tell her something about the man she just arrived with? Was it an omen? Marcus swept into the room behind her; she jumped, and then he pinched the skin at her waist. *Isn't this something? Bet you ain't seen anything like this before. I got this for you, babe. Now don't say I ain't done nothing nice for you.* She excused herself to go to the bathroom, marble and larger than the apartment she had been living in. Contorting her body around, she looked in the mirror, saw that where Marcus squeezed, a bruise was forming.

In an effort to conserve, we encourage you to reuse your towels and linens. If you would like them replaced, please place them in the bathtub.

He knew his mother would be home soon. He knew she didn't respect boundaries. He knew she would spit, toss a towel at him, and make him say at least fifty Hail Marys if she caught him. And still, this newly discovered habit brought him an almost yogic peace. He thought about Amanda, his girlfriend who had been a whole year older. She was a sophomore. She did things like blow in his ear like she was trying to cool him off. She did things like slip notes to him through the vents at the top of his locker. She did things like say she was never ever, ever, going to have sex until she got married. She did things like create crossword puzzles with secret messages to him. She did things like promise she could never go for Zack. She did things like forget their date at the ice cream parlor. She did things like not text him back. She did things like get pregnant. She did things like disappear for a few weeks. She did things like never meet his eyes again. She did things like that. And he did things like think of her in those moments when his body still needed her.

Monica didn't have enough money to buy new towels. The monogram was a bruise that wouldn't fade. In slick baby blue cursive: MEK. Kevin had left and now she was just ME, which was so literal she couldn't help but laugh. But she couldn't pull off the K without also taking the M and the E. She decided to only use the side of the towel that was not monogrammed. After time, only the one half of the towel shredded away, disintegrating with use. On the other side, as if it was the day of their wedding, were letters she didn't even recognize anymore, despite their gentile perfection.

You rub your daughter's hair dry, and a minuscule louse peddles away on the white terry cloth.

Rena had two towels. This was one more than she had ever had in her life before. This was also her first visit to The Club. She garnered a guest pass as a tip at the bar where she waitressed nights. Rena knew she had to bring a towel and understood the grungy, now-gray towel that barely covered her thighs, the one that she had filched from the school pool where she was a substitute teacher, would not be a wise choice. She knew that. She also knew she needed to wear a swimsuit. Picked from a bin also at the school pool, she poured herself into the Lycra. A few extra rolls bubbled at the seams, but it was a comfortable fit. She could cover the Wissahicken Warriors logo with a casually placed arm. What she didn't know was quite a lot. Would food be provided?

Was she going to be assigned a spot to park herself? Would people stare at her? Is she supposed to just leave the towel and her things as she went into the pool? Was it okay that she didn't know how to swim? What if she saw students from school? Would they even know her, her presence so occasional, so in-consequential, did they even see her when she was right in front of them in the classroom? She decided to bring the burgundy and white striped towel, the one she bought at Goodwill. It was in excellent shape with a small insignia sewn into one corner. It was very soft and rather large. Rena too had gone very soft and rather large, and felt this was the perfect cover for her in her swimsuit on her first day visiting the swimming club.

65-gram Egyptian cotton with double-rolled, hand-sewn scalloped edges.

A bird flies into the window. With a thump that stirs you from your dish-washing reverie, you see a wet smudge on the newly cleaned window. You go outside to find a robin laying at the base of the house. One wing twitches and goes still. Its coal eye reflects your own fatigued face. You holler for help, refusing to tear your sight from the bird's eye. On your watch, it dies. Your husband brings a towel and with rubber dishwashing gloves, you pick up the avian corpse. The robin's breast is a deep copper, not red like the songs say. It is buried in the towel at the base of your Japanese maple tree. The leaves are the same color as the bird's chest and when the wind rustles the leaves, you like to think you can hear the bird singing.

Emily, Beside Herself

Emily was beside herself. Literally, beside herself. She wasn't sure what happened, or how it was even possible. One minute she was on the 2 Train sitting between a woman reading *The Alchemist* (cliché) and a business suit with a cell phone clipped to his belt. (Also, cliché. Also, tacky and gauche). The next minute she was sitting between the suit and herself. Dressed in the same ill-fitting skirt, with the same earbud wires spilling out of her ears. (Don't tell anyone, they weren't actually attached to anything. Emily held the end in her pocket.)

Emily had just been fired. "Millennial," they accused. Indignant, she used one arm in one swoop to clear her off desk, stomped out saying they'd regret it. She pulled down her ironic kitten-hanging-on-a-branch poster (she told anyone who came into her cube it was meant to be a joke) and left it curled on the floor. Kicked over the trashcan and then put it upright again.

So as Emily sat next to herself on the train, she wanted to say to the person who looked just like her: *Who are you?* and *Did you also screw the fuck up?* But since she also didn't want to talk to anyone, she was unsure that this was really something she wanted to do.

In her lap was a bag with a broken handle. It was filled with the things that had been on her desk (picture frames with stock photos of happy people, an extra sweater knit for her by her mother, an award: *Team of the Year!* etched in Lucite, a musk candle, and a selection of essential oils).

The train jostled to a stop between 72nd Street and 96th Street. Almost home. And Emily thought, her other self was also almost home. Should she invite her in? She had never invited anyone in, except for that one man, that one time, that one terrible, broken time, and then never again.

Announcement: *track work; a delay.*

The other Emily looked up at the advertisements. Emily followed her gaze. Fix your skin. Fix your breasts. If you see something, say something. Fix your smile. Emily wondered who she should say something to. No one else noticed the identical women. And Emily was sick of men telling her to smile.

Emily looked at herself. The same frayed cuticles, bitten nails. The same pockmarks and heavily watered eyes. Emily always looked like she was about to cry, but that was just her face. Though it was true, she was always about to cry.

Someone then began to sing. It was not Emily, or Emily's doppelganger. It was just some guy singing just some ballad about love. Most of the people on the train ignored it. A few looked up and smiled the thin-lined smile of the appeased.

It wasn't long before the other Emily rose to her feet, reached for the bar overhead, pulled out her earphones, and slowly started to sway. Emily would call it dancing, in fact. In short time, Emily wanted to be this other Emily and not herself and drop all the baggage – the stuff she stole and what was taken from her – but she couldn't bring herself to even smile. Eventually she extended a hand. Emily refused. The song ended, and the musician walked up and down the train car, saying nothing, just nodding with an upturned hat in hand. Emily was not going to give this guy money for entertainment she didn't ask for.

Emily didn't dance. Not when people were looking. The man began another song, one she didn't recognize. She watched as the other Emily gained an audience. And then other voices started to sing (off-key). Seemed everyone else recognized the song and at the chorus, she did too. Emily recalled the words and remembered her mother's bedside radio, perpetually on. She hadn't seen her mother in a year because *life is sooo busy in the city*. Two hours to Bucks County seemed too long, and her mother would know what had happened just by looking at her.

The train exhaled, lurched. Soon the doors opened at 96th Street. The singer got off. Everyone plugged in their earbuds again, looked down at their phones. Dancing Emily got off. Emily stayed in her seat, transfixed by the sudden return to normalcy. It wasn't until 125th Street that she realized she had missed her stop.

But the other Emily, she knew better and had gotten off at the right place.

Some Sort of Apology

Mother, may I? Mary, may you? Heavenly father. Someone. It was the first time. My very first, swear. We were in Nevada. Okay, Vegas. I wear the penitence around my neck like costume jewelry I once thought was beautiful. Sometimes people ask me if it's real. I won't ever tell. Sometimes I don't even know myself. They say you can tell by the weight of the thing. I could wear this into shallow waves and drown myself, so I think they're wrong.

I lost it. I wore it to a concert. It was loud. Crowded. Beer soaked, hazy-something-like-love in the air like smoke from a wildfire – makes sunsets incredible, but poison fills your lungs as you gaze lazily upon the beauty. I could feel sticky fingers pulling at my pockets, my wrists. Tugging, kissing – acts that confuse the line between love and hate. Everyone wanting a piece of me.

Someone probably stole it, the fake jewelry – that reproduction of something pretty and valuable – supposing it was real. I feel lighter now, but I wonder: Is it around someone else's neck, weighing them down? Did they know, when they put it on, carefully clasping it in the back, laying it just so on their body? The funny thing is that, like a ghost limb, I can still feel it sometimes. Knocking against my chest, heavy on my heart. But these days, I can go days without thinking about it. I've stopped going to church.

The Inevitable Breaking of Limbs

So it's September, and it's one of those nights you know is going to be the last, but you never really know, you know? The pea soup city heat seeps in through uneven windows and he's got your arm all bent backwards. So far, it's ok.

It's usually ok. It aches where he twists the skin on your forearm and the elbow joint gets a little kinked, but it's ok. It doesn't break. This time it doesn't break.

And later, you will grovel and apologize with your husband's name stuck behind your tongue; you can't quite get it out and you sometimes wonder if it's because you don't lie. Not even white lies. Your mother never liked you for that. Her casseroles were too wet, or too dry and they lived on the roof of your mouth for hours.

Your husband doesn't like when you do that. Cry, that is. The tears emasculate him, he says. Your tears make him feel like less of a man, and you find it fascinating that a little salt water can be so powerful. If by "less of a man," he meant he'd be a lighter load, then maybe you'd have tried to drown him when you visited the Dead Sea last summer – a whole figurative ocean of tears.

It was a trip to the Holy Land and had been a gift from your mother-in-law. You almost thought it was an apology; a "sorry the baby thing didn't work out, but here's this life-changing experience" kind of thing. You weren't religious. You just called the place Israel, but she was all evangelical and, anyway, maybe you thought it would save you. You were Jewish once. But that fell by the wayside somewhere around fifth grade. Never even had a Bat Mitzvah. And, along with your classmates, you could sing Jesus songs like the best of them. This was why your in-laws didn't mind you so much. Also, you think, they too thought they could save you.

Before the flight took off, you took Dramamine and wore tight, terry-cloth bracelets on your wrists meant to keep you from growing nauseous. For the eleven-hour plane ride, like his name, you kept it all back, though it was not easy – your body all bent up into ridiculous angles and astringent bile collecting in your throat. Your husband closed his eyes on take-off and didn't open them until the plane landed at Ben-Gurion airport. You were in the window seat and you didn't dare move. By the time you were in the Holy Land, you were sweating something monstrous, and he said he felt shiny and rested. Shiny. He said shiny.

You floated in the Dead Sea. Everyone floats in the Dead Sea. But what they don't tell you, is that you shouldn't shave the morning of. A million sea lice nipped at your pores with poison or so it felt. You visited the wall and Galilee and the shuk and Yad Vashem, the Holocaust Museum. He cried, you noticed, when he saw all of the shoes. The thousands of shoes that weren't even matched up, just piled in peeling mounds of leather. You held it together until you entered the Children's Memorial, a hall of a million and a half lights, all representing a child killed at the hands of the Nazis. And when you heard a ghost whispering *Sophie*, your knees buckled.

That was going to be the name of your child, but after the non-breaking of limbs, but after the tassel-loafered kick to the gut, Sophie instantly gushed into what you likened to a red sea, but in Eilat, you saw that Sophie didn't resemble the Red Sea at all. She was not a Mediterranean and hopeful blue. You know that you should have known better. The Red Sea wouldn't be red. You suffered from cramps for months.

This time, on this humid night, as you sniffle and apologize to your husband, a rumble of thunder rolls outside like the voice of God. The tall branches outside your window sway and bob, marauding shadows marching out to greet him. You don't believe in God, but when the storm whips up and the power goes out, your husband loosens his grip. The branches begin to scratch at the window. He lets go. They snap off, one by one, and hang in the air for the briefest of seconds before they fall down, down, down and out of view.

The branches all break off. He goes into the bathroom. You grab your bag – the one you had stashed in the closet for emergencies – the one he thought was your gym bag, but you don't belong to a gym – and leave. The tree just looks like a skinny pole and at its feet are the fractured, useless limbs. So is the nature of a late summer storm.

And you think maybe you could believe in God. If you had to.

Mise en Place

A teaspoon of salt. It is flaky and the flakes overrun the tiny spoon, and the recipe calls for kosher, but the only thing in my cupboard is the fancy kind from France bought at the organic grocery store. Already I'm doing it wrong.

On my counter, I have in various-sized bowls:

- ¼ cup flour
- Carrots (2) – julienne
- Onion – small dice
- Sweet potatoes (2) – large dice
- 1 cup chickpeas
- 1 tbsp paprika

and a few strands of saffron, sitting delicately in a white ramekin. The strands are small and fine like microorganisms, they are potent despite their size. If I look through a microscope, I wouldn't be surprised if they are actually alive.

A prepared chef is a good chef, my mother used to say, her words filling her mouth, thick and spicy-sweet like the apricots in the tagines she made on Sundays. She's been dead for three months, and I hate cooking. But for my father's seventieth, I'm giving it a try. He misses my mother. She cooked a lot. I don't.

A few hours later, he is first to arrive. I seat him in the lounge chair that used to be his – leather, the color of the yolk of an over-boiled egg. When they upgraded to the beach condo, my mother said they had no use for it and replaced it with the stabby discomfort of wicker. I think he still mourns.

I don't have turmeric. The food will not have the golden hue that says: this flavor will be so deep it will evoke Marrakesh or Fez, or even the urban every-city-ness of Casablanca, where my mother and father met. Instead, I'm sure it will say: *welcome to Fridays, can I take your order?* So, nostalgic in its own way, but not what I'm going for.

Len and Paula, and the single brother, Joseph, finally arrive. They come together, disgorging from a country-sized vehicle. It's Len's and he said they needed it for all their children, but they never had kids.

"Oh my god," Paula, my sister-in-law, says. "We were just watching *Law & Order: S.V.U.* in the car."

"Oh my god," I repeat, unsure what God has to do with it.

"I could watch that show for hours," Paula says. "In fact," she giggles like a confessing teenager, "we sat around the corner for the past twenty minutes cuz we just *had* to finish the episode."

"How can we help?" Joseph asks, coming in behind Paula.

"Cut this onion," I say. And it isn't two chops later that he is crying. Makes two of us.

I had already set the table, and I have no need for any more chopped onion.

"What is this?" Len asks.

"Assigned seating," I say. There's grumbling, and I see Paula move her name card.

I put out the food. Cured meats in crenellated folds; cheese: brie, goat, and manchego; crudité; eggplant and tomato salad; store-bought *bourekas*; the stew; and some homemade burnt *khobz*.

"What, no couscous?" Joseph says smiling.

"Well, *petite soeur,* trying to be mom?" Len asks, and instantly puts his napkin to his mouth, as if trying to catch his words. Too late. There is silence. Loud sips of water. Folding and refolding of napkins. I'm thinking about a response and instead find myself thinking of a joke my mother used to tell, something involving an elephant and a jar of jellybeans – I can't recall the details and now I'm craving licorice jellybeans.

A film is forming over the stew. The carrots on the veggie tray are sweating. Paula fidgets. My father, who has moved the non-condo worthy chair over to the table, despite its size, heaves a loaded breath through his nose. It causes the flame on the candles to flicker. This house could burn down, I think.

"Dig in," I finally say. They do. Paula whispers that the stew is bland. Len says it's just like mom made. I go back to the kitchen. Bring out the pepper grinder and salt. I only eat the prosciutto and bresaola, shoving piece after piece of thin saltiness onto my tongue. I scrape charred flakes from the *khobz* onto the white lace tablecloth – a wedding gift to my parents, now a worn hand-me-down of mine – another beach-condo casualty. I look over to see my father tracing the lace design with his fingers.

No one gives a toast and I forgot to make dessert. No one sings happy birthday, though everyone mutters it to my father as they leave.

Later, we load the egg-yolk chair into my pick-up. I drive my father home. Install the chair in front of the TV.

"Happy Birthday," I say as I kiss him on the cheek – a brush of my lips on his leathery cheekbone, almost his eye.

"I hope there are leftovers," my father says – a kindness. I hold up the containers filled with food. He nods and picks up the remote, reaches for the lever to recline the seat.

In the kitchen, I hear the TV go on – the news. The endless, hopeless news. As he settles in, I make him some tea and put the leftovers in his fridge, enough for the week, maybe more.

The Gargoyles Survey Their City

They were the last of their kind in the city. What were they still doing there? They asked this of each other daily. High above, the two gargoyles surveyed the terrain below. Unlike the humans, they were unable to leave, tethered there by the masonry of grand edifices and equally grand hubris. Most of their kind had crashed down over the years, leaving behind a single claw or a broken wing – the only hints of what was once there.

It was a bank. Or a hospital. Or a department store. It didn't matter. The gargoyles had not shopped there. They were only meant to keep watch.

And they did.

They watched when the people were pushed out and when the fires and when the weeds and when the guns and when the urban mountains the people insisted on scaling fell. They watched. And they couldn't do anything.

High above the detritus of this once-city, the gargoyles were still beautiful. Or hideous. Or something in between. They

Were half animals – chimeras; they were monsters; they were cherubs. They weren't much different from the people who lived there.

They have survived the winters – the vicious cold that snapped branches and metal pipes, stole breath and never gave it back. The gargoyles sat sentinel where they were placed a century before.

The gargoyles talked to each other, as they had no one else to talk to. They wondered if their city would rise from the dead. One of them didn't believe in that kind of thing, said the legend of the phoenix was bullshit. Another was hopeful.

Far below, a shopping cart was pushed along the road by a great gasp of wind. A phantom family with cereal and boxed macaroni and cheese and toilet paper. In the front basket, a baby sat and cooed and giggled. The gargoyles called the baby Fred and wished they could tickle its chin. The ghost mother pushed the cart all the way home, even though that wasn't the way it worked, back in the day, when a supermarket filled in the blank space across the street. The carts were not meant to leave the parking lot.

One of the gargoyles called out to warn the mother of the broken glass beneath her feet. *It will cut her all up,* one gargoyle told the other. *She isn't real,* it was reminded.

A truck pulled up. Several. *Have the people come back?* the hopeful gargoyle asked. Along the side of the truck, where the gargoyles couldn't see, it read "Demolition Dudes" and they had come to ransack the buildings that were left. To take the fireplaces and the copper and all the things that were considered valuable. The gargoyles had seen that kind of thing before.

They watched as a crew carried out tools and machinery. They imagined them coughing in the dust. Maybe reminiscing about their childhood. Did their fathers bring them here for a day at the office? Did they visit the museums? Walk in the parades?

But none of these people were from the area. And when they took their sledgehammer, first to the hopeful gargoyle, they did it from behind, mercifully, so it didn't have to watch.

The Last Time They Came.
The First Time I Understood.

So I said, "Nurse, what are you playing at?"

And she said, "Alexander, I'm not playing at anything, they're coming today." I knew she was wrong or lying. I took the pills she offered, those teeny tiny bricks and popped 'em back. "I don't need water, Bridget," I said when she offered.

Mike and Diane said they were coming today. Bringing the kids – probably bribing them with candy or a car trip to Chuck-E-Cheese. Libby was named after my Elizabeth and Sasha, named after me, but I'm not dead yet so there's that. Jewish tradition says you don't use the name until the namesake is dead. Sasha is eleven so Mike and Diane had high hopes pretty early, I guess.

I asked Bridget to sneak in some Milano cookies. "You're diabetic," she told me, but she brought them anyway: mint, raspberry, and orange. I love the way the buttery cookie gave way to the chocolatey inside. The perfect cross section of horizontal lines when broken in half. The snap of each bite. I arranged them on a plate, red roses curling around the edges of the porcelain. Elizabeth's china. Well, ours, but she picked them out. I fan the cookies outward. Elizabeth would've been proud.

I shuffle toward the bathroom, the doorway surprisingly tight for a place like this. I tie and retie my bow tie. Haven't worn it in ages, not since my sales days, door to door, Bethesda to Buffalo to Amagansett. East Coast Best Salesman, 1956. Anyway, Bridget has to help me with my bow tie on days like these.

"You look handsome, Alexander."

"Call me Sasha," I tell her. I want to wink, but don't.

"Call me Meg," she says.

I wait. They're supposed to arrive at 11:00. The clock shows 11:04. I stand in front of my door covered with artwork from when the kids were really young. Scribbles, doodles, and stick figure family portraits: Mom, Dad, Grandpa, Libby, Sasha, and Minx, the dog. I had a full head of hair back then, depicted as a red Medusa with strands standing upward from my scalp. So weird for your kind, they'd always said. Sure you're not Irish, I was asked, as I ran up and down the alleys of the Lower East Side. A list of counties dribbled from the tongues of women who missed their homes. No, not from Cork. Not from County Kerry either. You haven't heard of it, I'd told them. It was true. Where I was from was no longer there anyway. Can you be from somewhere that disappeared?

11:11, this was the time my mother said to make a wish. So I did.

11:17, surely, they've just hit some traffic. I help myself to a cookie, they leave melted chocolate lines on my hands. I lick it off like I'm a child.

11:33, I feel the sugar. My heart a hummingbird; they're so beautiful. Elizabeth used to mix up nectar water for them and hung feeders in the yard. I press my hand to my chest to feel her. Sweat forms on the skin under my bow tie, and I try to loosen it with my fat fingers. Thick and clumsy, I pull the wrong side, tightening it around my neck and feel I might choke.

11:40, my knees ache. My back protests this stupidity. *Sit down. Lie down, rest up,* my joints say. I listen and get into bed. It's one of those mechanical contraptions, so I can use the remote to sit up when they arrive.

12:02, the phone rings. I must have dozed off. I answer. I know I sound groggy.

"Dad? Dad, is that you? I can't even understand what you're saying. We can't come today. Sorry. Sasha has a soccer game and Libby's got a bit of a cold. Ok? Next time. Ok, Dad?"

I hear the suction *slap, slap, hiss* from Arnold's room next door. *Slap, slap, hiss.* The syncopation is beautiful, and I begin to tap my finger on the phone receiver along with the beat. Arnold's been on that machine for at least a year. It'll be the last sounds of his life and I doubt he even hears the music.

"Dad? Dad, are you there?" My bow tie has fallen to the ground and I've eaten all the cookies.

The Intimacy of Brushing Teeth

They meet in the bathroom. It's only 9 o'clock and they are beginning their nightly routine. It will not take more than fifteen minutes, ten, five. She wants the day over already, and so, even though she is not tired, she will go to bed. Lay her messy mat of curls on her pillow and lament that she hasn't done the wash in over a month.

He will brush his teeth with his mouth wide open, sea foam dripping, great big white horse teeth open and wide, and abstract art-like sprays of toothpaste mar the mirror and the wall and the faucet.

The next night:

They meet in the bathroom. She says she needs privacy. Why do you need privacy? I want to floss. Floss here. Do it here. In front of me. No. What do you need that I can't give you, Elise?

What? (And here we learn her name, but not his. Not yet. Is it important to the story? Possibly.)

The following night:

They meet at eight o'clock. Without saying anything, they agree that the earlier they can go to sleep, the better. Some might call it avoidance, but she has collected – printed, snipped, saved – several articles on the benefits of going to bed early, if anyone should ask.

No one has asked.

She had wanted a double vanity, but when they were looking at houses, their budget said, nope. No double vanity. No granite counters. No garage, just a carport. The realtor looked at them with pity. And also, your shower will be made of plastic and you will have one bathroom in the entire house. (The real estate listing said ¾ bath, so not even a whole bathroom.) That is what you can afford and that is what you will have and that is indeed what they ended up with. So that now, in the space of their tiny bathroom, in the fug of overripe-pear-mildew, they brush their teeth at the same time. Now, of course they could take turns, but they decided to go to bed at the same time and it had not occurred to them otherwise. Elise could say, I will now put on my pajamas, then I will brush my teeth and wash my face, etc., etc., etc. He can feed the cat. The cat's name is Lars, and he too joins them in the in the bathroom, sitting on the back of the toilet, waiting to be pet on the head, or scratched behind his ears. But they arrive in the bathroom at the same time. This is the program for the evening: brush teeth, wash face, put on pajamas, feed cat, sleep.

It is Tuesday. They will have sex.

Their mouths will taste like peppermint. He likes this and she does not. In fact, she would rather not kiss at all. Just get it done with. Then, she can proceed with laying her head on the unwashed pillowcase, on the pillow stained with who knows what. She tries not to look when she changes the sheets. Does all that come from her? Her mouth? Is it her brains oozing out? Why are the stains on the pillow yellow? Really, more of a light rust color; is she rusting away? Her own saltwater turning her body into flaking metal?

Bernard is coming. Bernard is moaning. (See, now it is time to name him, and did you not expect "Bernard?") Bernard is handsome and able to come just by thinking about a Big Mac. Bernard is younger. He was considered the catch in the relation-ship, and Elise didn't know about catch and release laws, so she kept him. This was a mistake, but only now looking at herself in the mirror above the dresser, only now seeing his baboon backside as he thrusts into her, only now tasting the mint – that encroaching weed – in his mouth, as he searches for her. She isn't there. She's in the mirror watching Bernard and the ur-Elise.

Wednesday:

They meet in the bathroom and Elise says she has to pee. Ok. So pee, Bernard says, as he spreads the toothpaste on his brush with the bristles flayed. He really needs to replace his toothbrush, Elise thinks, but doesn't say. She's not his mother. Elise says, never mind, I don't have to go, and with his toothbrush sticking out of the side of his mouth, Bernard pulls down his pants and takes hold of his penis and pees. Hole in one, he says triumphantly, which Elise can't quite make out on account of the toothbrush in his mouth, but she knows what he said. He says it every night. Has done so since their honeymoon, after a long day of him out golfing and her at the spa. He spent seven out of eight days golfing while they were on the Yucatán Peninsula. He regaled her on his day and how he got a hole in one with his new friends Mark and Andy, and he was peeing at the same time and the irony of that meant his joke would go on for years. Eight years now.

In any domestic tragedy, we see ourselves. Where do you see yourself? Are you the catch? Are you the one who planned the honeymoon, and did he say he didn't care where you went, as long as you were together? Do you have a bathroom with a double sink? Do you have two sinks, but live alone?

Bernard and Elise will be married for twenty-two more years. He will die first. Many will attend the funeral. Elise refuses to say anything, to eulogize. Everyone thinks the sadness is too much to bear.

The night of the funeral:

Elise brushes her teeth alone. She picks up Bernard's toothbrush – not the same one from two decades prior, but still it needs replacing, again, always. She throws it out in the trashcan under the sink. Then, after she flosses, she plucks the toothbrush from the garbage and runs her fingers against the bristles. They're still a little damp. She runs it against her cheek. It's cool and tickles. She likes the feeling. She's going to let it dry first, she decides. In bed, she looks at herself in the mirror. Her body takes up less than half the bed. It feels like an enormous bed, a big luxury, that she alone has such a large bed.

Yolk

In the kitchen, I find Clara by the sink, looking out the window. Still. Dozens of eggshells are scattered along the granite counter. Broken in halves, segments, shiny egg whites hang off jagged edges. The morning light falls across Clara's messy braid, making her hair look almost red. But she shifts, and her hair is brown again.

I want to apologize for last night, but I can't seem to shape my mouth in that big O required for Sorry. Instead, I say, *making breakfast,* but she says nothing. I move to her side and look at her face to see what – if – she is looking at, and I see a drip of yolk threatening to spill off her chin. She is chewing, and she chews and chews, and it looks like she has raided a hen house.

She notices me, maybe, and says, "the eggs." She looks down at her hands as if meeting them for the first time. "The eggs have all gone."

"Gone?"

"Gone bad."

It is then I notice that there are broken eggshells in her hands. At her feet. Yolk painted across her shirt like modern art. There are shards in her hair too. I can tell from the way she stands – one foot out to the side, knee bent, hip resting against the counter – that her back still aches from carrying the baby even though she no longer is.

Clara woke early to make a strata. Eggs, bread, milk, a vegetable or two. Something lush for Jonathan on his first day of his new job. Last night didn't go as planned and she just wanted to make everything right again. The spinach was browning along the edges, and the carrots were limp. But they could still be used, right? Six months ago, she had taken maternity leave; he had lost his job. She was still on leave – unpaid – and wasn't sure how she could go back. The people in the office knew, of course, sent her a dozen roses – which seemed a weird flower to choose for death. Her out-of-office still said *"I'm having a baby! Be back in three months. If you need help, please contact Marie at..."* Clara sent emails to her office email at least five times a day just to read the message.

Once Jonathan got the new job, she assumed things would get better. When they got news of the position, she bought some lingerie – a deep burgundy silk. She had to struggle to get her post-partum body into the gauzy bra and matching panties – which felt extra cruel. But Jonathan had a penchant for lacy things, so she traced the stretch marks with her fingers as she positioned herself in what might pass as sexy on the bed, waiting for Jonathan. She fell asleep to the sounds of the TV downstairs – some 24-hour news channel talking about tragedy.

Things between them had become tense long before that unbreathing child slithered from her, that tiny body all blue-white in vernix and slippery with blood. Bank accounts had dwindled, and Clara was nesting: white wooden crib, organic mattress, polka-dotted sheets, onesies with stripes – always and only stripes, she had decided – at least for the first six months, and a moon-shaped nightlight. Jonathan grumbled and sighed when he eyeballed the credit card statements. She stood ready for defense, but he never said anything.

Now, several months later, Clara had cracked an egg into a clear bowl and immediately released a sob. There, in the golden yolk, she found the curved body of a baby chick – an embryo, really. It was scrawny and flimsy, all curled into itself. Clara's breasts began to leak as she pulled away the viscous goop with a fingernail, taking care not to harm the creature. She laid a clean dishtowel in a plastic storage container and then placed the little corpse in it, like a bed. Like she was tucking it in, and she thought, yes, I could've done this. I could've done it well. See how I didn't cover its mouth. See how I placed its head down first, softly, so softly, and then followed with the rest of the body?

She cracked another egg and found a minuscule stroller. Another egg, and she found a bottle – she was only going to breastfeed, she had thought. Another egg, a pacifier – blue. She washed it under the faucet and closed one eye looking through it. It made everything take on an aqua hue, like she was underwater. She placed that too on the counter. *Crack, crack, crack.* The collection grew: booties – wet from the yolk, the smallest book – pages warped with moisture, jar of baby food. All the things a baby would need, things she had also bought for her own child.

She cracked open another egg, banging it first on the counter, then cracking it in half, discarding the shell, holding the yolk, allowing the whites to drip between her fingers. There she discovered a small diaper. It was heavy due to the wetness of the egg. She had forgotten diapers. She was going to bring her baby home and didn't even have diapers yet. *Shit*, she thought. *What kind of mother am I?*

With one swoop of her arm, she wiped all the things away, off the counter, into the sink. Flip went the garbage disposal switch – *churn, churn, churn.* The sound of metal stuck in metal. She ran the water – she heard you were supposed to do that. Help things go down better. Her hands were covered in egg whites and yolk and she felt everything was slippery. She brought her fingers to her mouth, tasted the metallic slickness on her skin.

———————

I touch Clara's back. She stiffens, then softens. When I place my two hands on her hips, she melts into me. I wipe her hands. When I see the small box with the baby chick, I say we will bury it. I say, I'll be right back, and go upstairs to put on my pants.

The hallway is dark, doors closed, curtains shut tight – as they'd been for the past few months. The one open door is to the nursery, and a small fractal of light issues into the darkness.

It is from the nightlight, the moon-shaped one Clara had gotten for the baby, and I allow it to guide me into the room. There I stand in a solemn darkness, seeing the outline of the crib and the mobile, turning slowly on some unseen and unfelt breeze. It is beautiful. It would've been perfect.

I open the drawer and pull out the folded collection of onesies, pocket the tiny socks. Pull the sheet from the crib and grab the plush monkey. I am unsurprised to find tendrils of viscous egg mixed up with bedding. Before I leave the room, I turn out the nightlight, pull open the curtains.

I startle when I notice Clara has made her way upstairs. I pick a small piece of eggshell, barely noticeable, from her chin. She turns the nightlight back on, says we may need it to see.

My Syllables

When you say, I'm sorry I can't pronounce this and look directly at me, I just say "present" and think I am giving you a gift. It is as if you think I am poisoning your mouth with my syllables. Your smile isn't apologetic, but the smile of a middle-aged teacher living two hours from the nearest Applebee's.

You scroll through the class names and not once do you stutter or stub your tongue on anyone else's name. This goes on every day. Allen, Barker, Smith, White. You eventually just skip over mine, look for me and nod when it's my name's turn.

Later, when you push that stubbed tongue down my throat, you still say nothing and I ask why not and you point at your mouth as if to say, I'm chewing right now, and I'll answer you once I swallow. I'm not a rude guy, you seem to be saying.

The janitors' closet is filled with all kinds of things. Not just bleach and mops and *Playboys*.

When you say all the girls like this, I say what girls, because where I come from – down the block – none of the girls would like this. We've talked about it – you – at the top of the slide, where we apologize to the little kids, but don't move. We only talked about it before, and we all agree that there's no way we would even. Now I barely go to the playground. It's for kids. But I can hear laughter echo from the top of the enclosed slide when I walk home. Sometimes I cross the street to avoid hearing that sound.

When you say it's our little secret, it's really not little. It's everything I can think of. It's melted solder in my veins trying to piece me together again, because maybe then I'd shine, and you could see me. And here, I made you something in art class. It's my stained-glass heart. You say it's pretty.

I want to talk to you about the smiley face you scribbled next to the B minus on my essay. Do you really think I don't understand what it's like to be a cockroach? I know what it feels like to be underfoot, an unwanted pest who skitters at the very hint of light. I know these creatures. They share the peeling linoleum and late-night brawls and empty vodka bottles with me and my mom.

When I tell you about it, you tell me I'm safe here. With you. In this closet. With all the poison. I start to wonder what "safe" means, and you take my face in your hands and I think I might know.

One day after class, you etch your initials into my desk, like a sixth-grade wannabe bad boy. As I walk out, my fingers brush another desk and find the splinters of your name. I check the desk next to it. And the one next to that. And the one next to that. I stay late to check and all the desks in all the rooms are branded by you, as if you own us all.

When you say if I tell… and pantomime a gun, your thumb the hammer, I wonder why. You said you loved me. Even though you don't say my name.

Trees Like a Way Out

All right, so I needed gas and rolled into the Sunoco practically on fumes and next to me was Bob Ross. And I'm like, hey, hey man, Bob? Bob Ross? He nodded. Look at those trees, I said. Tell me about those trees, and Bob Ross was like, I'm just filling my gas, friend.

He was filling up with Premium. Must be something, to live like Bob Ross. I ran into the food mart quickly, keeping my eye on Bob through the window. I slapped down a ten on the counter. Pump three please. Under the harsh lights and amidst the aroma of slowly churning hot dogs I realized maybe I was dead, and this was a kind of way station to heaven and Elvis and Jesus would pull in any moment. Gran always said she saw Jesus in things: toast, tea, Target.

I ran back out and selected the cheapest gas. Bob Ross was at the pump next to mine and his car was a 1985 Plymouth Voyager. You know the minivan? The one with the wood paneling along the side? It was just like my Gran's living room – minus the crystal bowls of Werther's and Precious Moments dolls. But the wood paneling. Sometimes it felt like those panels were prison bars. She eventually had the paneling taken down, and after that I'd push my cheek up against the cold plaster of the wall and feel free and soothed, but like something was missing. Gran raised me after my parents left, together. I spent hours watching PBS while my grandmother knit in the corner. She made scarves that never ended. She didn't say much except to say the following things: Are you capable of anything? What do you want to be when you grow up? Why don't you apply yourself in school? But then, once she gave me some paints and a book of fancy paper just because. She'd run her fingers along the paint when it dried and pulled her lips into a line and said she liked my use of textures

One of my first paintings was of a great big tree with a nest of robins in a high branch. Robins don't nest that high up, Gran said, but she hung it on the fridge anyway, where it still hung, nearly twenty years later, hidden beneath coupons, childhood school photos of my mom, and reminders of doctors' appointments long passed.

I said, hey, Bob Ross. Your car reminds me of my Gran, and he was all offended and I was like, no, no, in a good way. You know those Precious Moments dolls? I said. With their eyelashes and cow eyes? he asked. Yeah, I said. Those. I didn't mean it like that, but I didn't think Bob Ross wanted to hear what I really meant.

Bob Ross was quiet for a moment and then was like, yeah. They were cute.

I loved watching your show when I was a kid, I said, toeing my shoe along some old gum, suddenly shy.

Thanks, he said and began to clean his windshield. Small rivers of dirt water fell off the ends as he completed one line then the next. Even finer strips of dirt were left on the windshield. It went dirt, clean window, dirt, clean window, so that when Bob was satisfied, he replaced the brush into the murky water bucket by the pumps. I looked at the not entirely straight lines in his windshield and thought, this was an artist.

He didn't say anything else, and I felt compelled to fill the space of silence. The trees, you know. The little trees, you made it seem so easy.

Yeah? He paced by his pump, his dollars ticking away behind him on the screen.

Yeah, in the end, just those little marks made everything so beautiful. That's art.

And I paused for a moment, heard the click of my own gas pump. Yeah, it is, he said.

Back in my car I realized: I just saw Bob Ross. I picked up my cell to take a photo, but the Voyager was gone. But I did notice a shiny rainbow puddle where the van had been, and believed it was beautiful, in its way, the way all toxic things are. I snapped a quick photo. Maybe I'd share it on social media. Gran just got a smartphone, so I zipped the image off to her and hoped she'd be able see it.

Mirror, ca. 1550 – 1350 B.C.

The item was cast in bronze in two pieces: the handle and the disk, the latter held the mirror. The item has been broken apart. (As if the subject of the reflection and the hand that held it are now separate.) Presumably there had been a rivet holding the two pieces, but it has eroded to a small nub. The disk is more oval than circular; there are imperfections in the shape which indicate the artifact was hand-formed. The mirror itself has been abraded to no longer reflect. It is simply something that is held up in front of one's face. (As if to hide.) On the back of the disk, hieroglyphics are too worn down and are indecipherable. (Perhaps once a name.) The handle is in the form of a stylized papyrus plant. Research has found this represents creative female power in Egyptian mythology.

It was found in a small coffin, as if for a child.

She closes down the museum's website, pushes her laptop away, stands. She wants to see it. But the catalog says it is not on view. She goes to the mirror in the hallway. Tucks an errant hair behind her ear, smiles the way she would to a child, to her child. She will be the only one to see this smile, the way she tilts her head and her eyes scrunch along the edges. Wonders if she can do it again, handle it again, wonders where and how she can pack away this mirror that has caught a mother in its reflection.

(It's not like Claire didn't bring it on herself.)

The indigo sky informed all of them that it would soon be time. That the children as clowns and superheroes and princesses would be stuffed full of Reese's and candy corn and rolling in their little beds positively asphyxiated with the sugar. The teenagers were dressed in threadbare tie dye tee shirts, fringed leather vests. Claire wore bellbottoms and a crop top. She had been about to pull on a long-sleeved shirt. (Ben said don't.)

Doris's house was not what you'd expect. A rambler, off-white brick and something that was not brick, but just as ugly. The numbers, 10220, hung off nails and threatened to drop, and then who would find her then?

It had been raining all week. Moisture clung to the blades of grass and ghost-fingered branches clasped above their heads, as if in prayer. Here the leaves and the apples had fallen early.

Above them, hundreds of crows sang their murderous song. Two blocks away, Eve Lake. If it were summer, they would hear the warble of frogs and have their skin lanced by mosquitoes.

Late night picnickers would be enjoying the ever sun. Today they could feel the future phantom of winter. Claire chewed her lips and picked at her fingernails.

Doris lived with her grandson Jake. Jake flicked his retainer in and out on his tongue and wore a leather duster that he said had been his father's. (His grandmother told him this lie, because he wouldn't wear a jacket otherwise.)

"I don't know if I really want to do this," Claire said.

The crows fell silent. Across from Doris's house, an automated eight-foot witch cackled. Marcus started humming and Ben added a low growly beatbox. The trio had been the standouts in *The One Notes*, the school's a cappella group. Claire added a high note.

"Shut up," Ben said.

Every year, a senior is selected as the lead. (Everyone said Jake was coming out of his shell and weren't they all so glad about that!?)

A gust of wind unfurled off the lake. A shrill bird.

"The fuck was that?" Ben said.

"An owl, what do you think?" Marcus said and slung the burlap bag over his shoulder. (It was not an owl.) The bag was already heavy. They shuffled along the driveway to the house.

Shiny wrapped candy waited in a bowl under the stuttering porch light. A shower was running and there was singing. (Jake was an excellent singer, but most people didn't know that.)

Ben's father had started *The One Notes* thirty years earlier.

At the front door, Marcus reached for a candy bar, but Ben slapped his arm back.

"Dude, they're Hundred Grands. We hit the Halloween lottery," Marcus said.

Claire wheezed and tried to control her breath, as if you could do such a thing, control the thing that keeps you alive. She thought about the kiss she and Ben had shared earlier that day. Under the bleachers at lunch, stealing a smoke, like always. But when she said, *fuck, it's cold*, Ben leaned over, locked his lips on hers, and exhaled the nicotine directly into her throat. She sputtered, and he put one hand up her shirt in an instant, the other still held onto his burning cigarette. When she finally got enough air to cough, he pushed her back. *Slut.* He laughed and Claire was unsure what had changed. The soft parts of her mouth still burned.

They had wandered back to the cafeteria, and he said he was looking forward to the auditions for the lead that afternoon.

That evening, on the dark side of the sun on Halloween by a lake, the teenagers stood with a bulky burlap bag at their feet.

"Do it," Ben said. Marcus rang the doorbell and they fled toward the lake.

No one came to the door. Claire was alone. She didn't see where Ben and Marcus had gone, but she had a straight view of Doris's door. She thought she saw movement. Her breath grew tight. She heard the creak of the door.

It was Jake, hair wet, slicked back, towel at his waist. Bare chest like snow in the night. He looked up and down the street (don't they always?) and only after a moment registered the bag. He nudged it.

Doris appeared over his shoulder. "What is it, Jakey?"

"A bag."

"Should we open it?" She didn't make a move to do so. "Is this from one of your friends?" (No.)

"You should've told them to come in," Doris said and went back into the house. She always wished Jake brought friends home. Jake stood there for a long while. Remembering a time before all this. A time when he didn't wear the not-previously-his-father's coat. (Yes, he knew.)

Jake undid the knot. Pulled at it to open the top. As he did, it frayed as if time moved forward. The bag released an overripe peach smell and he pulled back the edges to reveal a tangle of long damp hair.

It was Claire. Claire in a bag, and her blond-brown wet hair and a red candy bar wrapper in her grip. Her eyes were closed.

Claire was always kind to him, saying *bless you* when he sneezed, smiling close-mouthed at him in the hall. Once she offered to get him a ditto from the teacher, so he didn't have to get up from his desk.

Was she breathing? He opened the bag, laid her legs and arms beside her body gently. Her limbs were still pliant; no rigor mortis at least. She was topless and he covered her breasts with the burlap.

Over the lake, the crows took off, hundreds of black smears in the sky. Two figures were running. Then the crows dove. Down, down, pulling at the hair of one figure, then the other, and then all Jake could see was one dark mass and he brought Claire inside.

The house was hot. His grandmother always had the heat on at 85, her collection of salt and pepper shakers covered every surface. Stifling. He felt trapped but wouldn't ever leave.

Claire's chest rose though her eyes remained closed.

We all are. (Trapped, that is.)

Swan Songs are Just Human Songs with Feathers

It was the off-season, and we were left to the rain that mourned the tourists. Paddleboats masquerading as swans. Swans masquerading as boats. Gone were the slushies and sunblock and *hey mom, can we ride these?!* Gone were the city stalwarts and country obese that brace us with their heft. Gone was the summer.

Except yesterday, a man and son came around. Knocked at the Waterfront Activity Center, but no one answered. The boy couldn't have been more than six. The dad, no more than forty, though his baldness shone bright even under the clouds.

"Sorry Max," the dad said, "they're all closed up."

"But I want to…" The boy began a windup that we were all familiar with. It would end in an alarm and we would be captive, tied up like this. The father kneeled, placed his forehead to his son's. Said nothing. The father hiked up his son, put him on his shoulders, and walked down the beach, leaving one set of footprints in the sepia sand. We could hear the suck of the water, the beach wanting to claim the last of life before winter. But the man wouldn't be taken in. We watched, as the two figures grew smaller and smaller. We felt relief, but also sadness.

One of us might have sung out.

Then, the man placed Max down. Hand in hand, they walked back in our direction. As they approached, the boy tugged off his sneakers and tromped towards the water.

"It's cold!" he hollered back.

"It is," the father said.

"You promised," Max said.

"I know," he said, "but these things happen." As he spoke, the winter ferry boat emerged from behind the cove. It trundled slowly but created large waves that formed whitecaps which bent into the beach where the boy stood. At first, he giggled. But on the fourth wave, he was soaked to the knees, and he tried to turn and run back to his father.

He yelled out. Fell. His father had been gazing into the distance and was unaware of the danger. Even the shallow waters hold monsters.

We could hear the boy call. For his father. For his mother. But it was only after he swallowed quarts of water that his father responded.

The man ran in, the water roiling but shallow, and pulled up his boy, who sputtered. And cried. And called again for his mother.

"I'm sorry," the father said into his son's neck, tasting the salty tang of grief.

We bowed our necks in sympathy. We too knew what it was like to be alone, in this vast, watery world.

We pushed each other toward the shore, toward the abridged family, nudging our plastic, feathered bodies into each other. Finally, one of us beached. And the son saw us, pulled at his father. We invited them in. We showed them our small piece of lake, of summer, of days that were better and not on the steady parade to winter.

Grovel

He stepped on her glasses and the crunch was the sound of a heart breaking. He had told her this was his experience, as a cardiac surgeon when wrist deep into someone's viscera. It echoed throughout the O.R., he'd said, and even the nurses shuddered.

At night, she studied his skin to find any staining from all the hearts, but he'd been sterilized, wiped clean.

Let me check your heart, I'm a doctor, he had said, in that bar in the decade where things mattered less, but everyone thought they mattered more. They replayed that moment over and over: engagement party, wedding, therapy, in her mind at that moment when her glasses were wrecked, and she couldn't see.

She had no more new contacts. The insurance expired after he lost his job. They didn't even extend it an hour. Fuck the administration. Fuck Babcock, he said. Sitting on the edge of the bed with her head in her hands, he paced. On each of his fingers, he listed someone else to fuck. She recalled a graveyard of pearly blue carcasses of dried-out contacts beside the bathroom trashcan that she could never be bothered to clean up. She left him pacing and closed the bathroom door. It smelled of bay rum and the hibiscus-like smell of mildew.

On her knees beside the toilet, she felt the tacky coolness, as her fingertips caressed the tiled floor. Tendrils of dead hair in whorls, the label of her Lexapro splatted on the tile like it had been glued there, the tossed aside stick of a pregnancy test – negative. Two contacts. Dousing them with saline, she knew it wouldn't help. She looked in the mirror and only saw a blurry smudge.

He came into the small room, encircled her waist, rested his chin on her shoulder, and she stared at the mangled image of themselves. The contacts were balanced on her fingertips, precarious as TNT. She jabbed one in her right eye, feeling the knife. She closed one eye and saw her and her husband more clearly. She then placed the other contact gently in her left eye. Maybe it would hurt less if she were more delicate.

She was wrong. She scrunched her eyes closed and felt every fine particulate that was too small to see, but irritated and would eventually, probably, cause her to go blind, or at least have irreparable damage.

"Here, let me see," he said and took her chin into his hand. "Bend down."

"No."

He let out a noxious breath through his nose. She felt the peeling of her eyes like an orange, the vitreous gel condensing.

"Open."

She opened.

"There's an eyelash." He brought his thick finger toward her eye. "Steady," he said. "Steady. Don't move." His wedding band dulled. She didn't recognize his fingerprints.

She flinched. He swore. Her eyes burned and burned and blurred until she couldn't even see him.

All Your Household Needs

The boy wanted a Lucky the Dog, but his dad said no. Lucky was a plush beagle who spoke when you pushed its paw. Lucky the Dog was the toy company's Hail Mary before the company tanked. Lucky would become bigger than just a plushie, the CEO said. He wore a suit. They all did, around an oval table filled with men.

A year after their decision, I was in a store that sold everything, and they didn't have what I wanted. So I went looking for Lucky. Some kind of confirmation that I was some kind of something. That the superstores, like this one, all over the country had me, a piece of me, in them and that would mean something. I was in one of the toy aisles when I heard the boy, when I heard his father, when I heard the familiar voice issuing from Lucky's speaker tucked neatly into its belly.

"Easy come, easy go." The boy had pushed on Lucky's paw. Other things Lucky said, but only when you took it home, unwrapped the plastic noose, and took it off trial mode: *I'm glad you took me home. Let's be friends. You can talk to me.*

I knew all this because I was Lucky. In the months after losing my baby at twenty-two weeks – the size of a spaghetti squash, an app told me – my agent called and said she had the best job for me. *I mean the best, Laura. Things are looking up!*

I auditioned and got the job as the voice of Lucky the Dog. At the time it was only a doll, but there were promises of an animated TV show, a touring stage production.

I tapped my foot on the linoleum to *Wham!* issuing from the speakers of the superstore.

Lucky was supposed to be this year's hit. The toy for which people would line up on Black Friday.

The father said, "This is a girls' doll. Are you a girl?" I didn't hear the boy's response if there was one.

Lucky was green and white. Intended to evoke no gender, or all of them. To vaguely suggest Christmas. At first, I heard sniffles, then sobs that I could tell were escaping despite the child's best efforts.

"Don't you fucking start with that."

The boy choked and coughed and said, "But Dad..."

And the father said, "Don't 'but Dad' me. Put that piece of shit down."

After several silent minutes, they entered my aisle. I pretended to look at a Barbie, tapered waist, blond. I looked at the boy who pulled his lips into a line.

"Can I look at these, Dad?" he pointed to the shelves of LEGO Star Wars sets.

"That's more like it." The man craned his neck toward the fishing supplies. "I'm going over there."

"Okay," the boy said with a catch in his voice.

I reshelved the Barbie and turned. "You can talk to me," I said, and the boy smiled in recognition.

What Goes with Us

Annie didn't see Leslie's last breath, because she'd bitten off a crescent of fingernail and was studying it, like it would give her all of the answers. Annie did not look into Leslie's eyes, wordlessly saying, *I'm here.* Annie did not say, *you are not alone.* Annie did not say, *I love you.* Annie flicked the nail and it landed in an open book – a library hardcover that Leslie had been reading before she couldn't anymore. The book had been read so often that the spine, like Leslie's body, had given up. It reminded Annie of a butterfly on display, or a woman's body open and ready to give birth.

She had told Leslie this when it first popped into her mind and Leslie rolled her eyes. *We didn't want kids.* You *didn't want kids. I know, I know,* Annie had said.

In the early months, Annie had watched Leslie in bed, vigilant to every change of breath, every possible ending. She rotated Leslie's body and read to her Rilke and Garfield comics. Turned on music in the early evening for softened, non-alcoholic happy hours. She had focused on every labored word from Leslie's parched lips, until those too tapered off. Months passed. Annie sought conversation from the hospice nurses and aids, and her mind reeled off to-do lists while she went through the motions and the accompanying dialogue, *turn, open up, hi babe, I'm here, turn again, this'll just pinch, open up,* and crushingly, *here comes the airplane.*

Annie thought she would've gasped and clutched Leslie's body when she died, envisioning wails and moans, prostrating herself to a God she didn't believe in. Instead, when she saw that Leslie's chest was no longer rising up and down under the quilt, she held her ear to Leslie's mouth, thought about how the proximity of these body parts once meant something else. She sat back down and stayed there for an hour, biting her nails even further down, as if she might find something there, underneath.

It was quick – too quick that Leslie's body was removed, the rented medical equipment whisked from the house, the book returned to the library. Annie wasn't sure if she did this, or someone else, so hazy was that time, the great yawn between relief, grief, and loneliness. The house was so quiet without the hiss of oxygen, or Otis Redding playing softly in the background.

After the funeral, Annie thought of the fingernail. It had been thick, difficult to pry off. It had gone too deep; it still smarted a week later. The nail had been bone-white and curved into a half moon, quarter, crescent, whatever. She once knew the phases of the moon – tracking them on the calendar with Leslie, going outside on clear nights. The mosquito bites worth it. The bats swooping in the trees overhead. Annie only knew Orion's belt, but Leslie seemed to know the positioning of every star. She could guide them on the seas, if they ever need it, Annie always thought.

Annie wanted the nail back. Proof of life in those dead skin cells. The last time it was attached to her body, Leslie had been alive.

What was the book? Annie logged into her library account. No, she hadn't taken a book out in four months it said. She missed when she had the focus, the ability to temporarily leave her own life in a book.

Of course, it would be under Leslie's account. She searched Leslie's purse, hands feeling around in the deep leather bag: Chapstick, bus pass with a sticker for a local ice cream shop on it, nail clippers – Annie laughed, a bone stuck in her throat. She eventually found the library card and put everything back, not wanting Leslie to lose the things she had needed once.

Annie looked up the account – Leslie's pin was their wedding date – so predictable that Annie's breath caught. Leslie had no overdue fines. Leslie had eighteen books on her "for later shelf," six books on hold, one in transit. The book that had been her last, Annie saw, was a scientific look at the afterlife. How appropriate, Annie thought.

At the library, Annie found the book easily and opened it exactly where it wanted to open, spine still soft, giving. Nothing was in the pages, which were leather-like and soft, but strong. She flipped through the rest of the book, shook it, loosening it from its plastic jacket. Her fingernail was not there. Proof of life, gone. She hoped that the cellular piece of herself went with Leslie wherever she went.

A librarian came over. "You can't treat the books like that."

"I know," Annie said. "Sorry." She sank into a couch and listened to the clatter of people on the computers. The smell of bread and human bodies unique to a library.

The librarian took the book from Annie's hands. "It's pretty beaten up."

"I'm checking it out."

"We can get another copy from another branch."

"No. This one's good,"

"This should be taken out of circulation," she said, and turned to a young man behind the desk. "Mike, do we –"

Annie snatched the book from the librarian.

The librarian looked back at Mike, for back-up perhaps, but he was already doing something else. The librarian kept looking around the space. Annie held the book tight. The zip of the copy machine, the clickety-clack of fingers on keyboards, a child's shout that was quickly silenced by their grown-up.

"I want this one," Annie whispered. With a fingertip, she pried an edge of the plastic cover up.

"We have a process for when the books get too worn," the librarian said, but she had softened. She was a librarian, because she understood the power of a book. "We probably have more copies. I can check for you."

"No, thank you." She pulled more of the protective cover off, gradually, trying to evade the librarian's scolding, though her destruction of the thing was in plain sight.

Mike rounded the desk.

"You need help?" he asked the librarian. The librarian sighed, then asked for Annie's library card. Asked for the book.

"Okay, you can take it," she said. "It's a good read." Annie handed it over. She then stared at her empty palms. The librarian scanned it. *Beep. Blip.* Handed the book back to Annie, who clutched it to her chest, allowing the loose plastic flap to tickle her neck.

She read it in a day. Didn't return it, let the fines accrue until the book was marked as missing. Paid the price. Let her fingernails grow.

The Jews' Things

The boat showed up sometime in the early morning hours. They think this because people who'd been promenading along the beach the evening before and the teenagers who were frolicking under the midnight moonlight had not seen it. So, it must have arrived in the dark, or the semi-dark, or the near lightness of day. Which is the way of such things, they said.

Though it's also possible they had just turned their heads away so as not to see.

It had been raining for weeks and there was a brief reprieve, which nearly everyone mistook for a change of season. Leon had come to the beach to see what he could find: agates, sea glass, solitude. He knew the weather would not last and it would storm again. In the sky an anvil of a cloud approached. Soon.

No one was aboard the boat, which was more like an oversized skiff. Piles of suitcases filled the space, precarious, but the dangerous balance had worked. The way things did until they didn't. These were all old things. Worn. Touched and packed and

122 / Jennifer Fliss

beloved. Leon thought of the word valise: a degeneration of
leather, faded tourist stickers, initials etched into the sides.

"It is the Jews' things," one reporter said, creasing his
eyebrows, his lips pulled into a grimace. Off camera he wiped
spittle away from the corners of his mouth.

How did they know it was the Jews' things? The items
looked as though they'd been decades at sea. Salt broke the locks
that had been placed so diligently on suitcases. Inside were things
the Nazis didn't bother, which was surprising given how they had
stocked their homes with the furniture of the Jews', placed upon
their walls the art of the Jews', lit their candles upon the candlesticks of the Jews', and filled the spaces that once were filled with
the Jews themselves.

Do these items still say *Jews* if there were no Jews left to
claim them?

It was not just the Nazis who had built homes out of the
Jews' ashes – their bodily dust the mortar, their belongings the
bricks. Leon knew this. It's why they lived in this small town now.
But his mother didn't talk about it.

No, this was something else, a cache that had in some
way, gone unobserved by the Nazis and the bystanders. This had
been allowed to escape. Only by the blessing that a human cannot
see everything. A forgotten thing. A hungry tide. A roiling ocean.
That was its safety.

On the beach, greedy hands pulled at the wrecked locks.
Inside Siddurs, shawls, mezuzot. Dresses, photographs, Kiddush

cups. The hands and reporters didn't know the names for these things, but Leon did.

Also inside were dolls made of fabric – hair tied in silky knots, novels, candlesticks, children's books, diaries, bow ties, skirts, socks that had been darned several times, and socks that looked new.

Somehow everything inside the suitcases had survived the sea. Leon did not believe in miracles.

A woman commented on the weird unfamiliar letters. A man fondled the silky strands of a doll's hair.

Leon had been beachcombing and he had seen the small boat a few feet into the water. He kicked off his shoes, rolled up the cuffs of his pants, and waded into the cold. There was a rope dangling, begging him to take it. It was heavy, all this baggage. He ran it aground after several attempts. It moaned, as it keeled to the left, the boat forging a deep indentation into the beach.

Its dreams had been lost, bobbing on the white crests of the ocean, at the bottom of the sea, probably further, back at its departure point.

The boat set itself upon the sand of this new land and decided yes, this will do. And there the boat filled with the Jews' things stayed until Leon found it.

He had made one phone call to his friend, who happened to be a journalist. Almost immediately, scores of people filled in around him. Everyone's always looking for treasure. Leon took several steps back and bled into the background.

The bright lights from the cameras. The puns uttered carelessly from the mouths of journalists. Leon regretted his call immediately. But there was nothing he could do. It was done. Leon thought how fitting it was. It was Friday evening.

His mother was making dinner right then. Roast chicken. Carrots with raisins. She did not make challah this week, but he had picked up some brioche – at her request – from the grocery store. Close enough; sometimes it was the best you could do. This Friday meal was special. The rest of the week frozen meals and takeout. His friends knew, but no one said anything. His mother had told him he should appreciate the gesture. *They don't often...* she had said, but not finished.

A joke about Anne Frank. A drop of rain on Leon's nose. Then two more. Sudden pockmarks darkening the sand.

Leon looked up. The items were packed into boxes and then into a van. Where were the things being taken? The beach emptied. Leon watched as the red rear lights faded into the night, as the van drove away.

Sand caught in his eyelashes, the grit nearly lacerating his corneas, but he did not look away.

The Great Bear

Working in Antarctica is for serious scientists, they say. For people who know what they're getting into. For people not like you, they don't say, but don't have to. They also do not say you are already so lonely we think the black cold of the tundra will kill you. They do not say these things, because a) It is implied and b) They do not think themselves cruel. They are Midwesterners and their cruelty lay in what is not said.

You're already partially made of ice, frozen so long ago that, if they drilled, they'd find the fossils of wooly mammoths. Furry, warm, but someone would have to brave the tusks first, and who'd be stupid enough to try that? The first known depiction of the constellation Orion was found on mammoth ivory. You love that those two things go together in that far off way.

When they do acknowledge your plans, they say you'll get eaten by polar bears.

You aren't leaving until May. You have five months and you're not sure you can make it here, staying in the town you grew up in, with your parents, in your childhood bedroom, under posters of bands you never liked.

These are the last holidays you'll spend in this cold midwestern town.

It starts to snow before they arrive. First the aunt and then the grandparents, and then the aunt and uncle and the many children. They doff their heavy coats and shuffle into the tight foyer. They drink old fashioneds and ask for extra cherries. The children go off to the plaid-carpeted and wood-paneled basement. Outside the window you watch the snow circle itself, a waltz.

Your degrees are just pretty pieces of paper with their curlicues, barely-legible scrawls, your full name in a serif font – so odd looking all together like that; you often think that it can't be you. You are not all those names, all those connections to the past, to your family. You are not married. Your fourteen years of experience in a lab are nothing, because you have no children. Fellowships, papers, commendations: feh, they do not say, but they also do not respond when you send your news via the family group text.

But oh, how they respond to your nieces' and nephews' photographs! In their Halloween costumes and first-day-of-school photos with the cutesy signs saying they want to be a doctor or scientist when they grow up. How cute, everyone replies-all with many exclamation points and emojis.

As you're staring out the window, someone asks if you're seeing anyone. They're entirely too close, and you can smell the whiskey on their tongue – a magic carpet of alcoholism. They have only just arrived, and their glass is still full.

Someone says their daughter is an asshole, then covers their mouth as if embarrassed, but they know what they said and are proud of it.

You know everyone's names, but don't recognize anyone.

The snow collects the way it does in the Midwest, at first on the hedges and then on the grass and then on the driveways and then on the street. They will all get snowed in, you think. They will all have to stay the night.

You open the screen door and step into the burgeoning snowstorm. You're wearing house slippers, but you don't care. You always pack your slippers. They will come with you to Antarctica too. You slide the door closed behind you into a silence only snowfall can elicit.

Overhead, outside of the city, you can finally make out some constellations. It is a small joy.

You look over at the shed where you had your first kiss: Mike McNeil. You wander over to the playset where you fell and broke your leg at eight. Halfway across the yard, you step wrong into a divot, and your ankle turns out. Fuck! You chastise yourself, because it's been there forever and how long has it been since you've been home that you could have forgotten? Your ankle radiates and feels tender, but it's okay.

Out here there are no fences to divide lots. Just expanses of grass between homes. In the day, you'd see playsets and statues of saints and dormant water features. In the dark, you see none of that, but you can feel their ghosts.

A rev of a truck out on the main drag. A second. Races, probably. It was big when you were a high schooler, though you never participated. Two kids died your senior year from such an event, but you can't remember their names.

Warm light emanates from the windows. A person walks across the field of vision in one window. A Christmas tree blinks in another.

In the house across the way, you see Ms. Horowitz sitting at her kitchen table. One of her hands holds up her head, as if it is so heavy it can't possibly stay up on its own. The other drums the table. She stares out the window and you wonder if she sees you. She was always so kind, volunteering in your elementary school library, offering you one book after another, recognizing a kindred spirit perhaps. One of the first books she gave you was a National Geographic book on animals in polar habitats. Behind her is a small light from above the stove; otherwise, her house is dark.

You recall when Mike – the one you first kissed – left a note with a swastika on it in her mailbox. He told you about it and giggled like he had left her a Valentine.

He never talked to you past sophomore year, and you hate that your first kiss was with a Nazi and that you can't erase that.

You keep walking. The snow whips around, beautiful, wild. Your feet are starting to get wet through your shearling slippers. Your thighs burn with cold. Your ears ring.

A laugh pierces the air – one of those animal guffaws that comes from a man who probably drinks a lot, was football captain, has two daughters with long hair, and bitches about socialism.

You hate it here. You always did.

So, you keep walking, past the backs of houses. These are the parts of houses that people don't want on display. Rusted lawnmowers, shipping boxes discarded in heaps, old cat beds, tangled pipes from who knows what.

For someone supposedly made of ice, you are getting quite cold.

The houses grow farther apart. You leave the festive lights behind and look up. There she is, Ursa Major, roaring up in the purple-black sky.

She guides you.

After what feels like hours, but it might've been ten minutes, wisps of clouds stream in. You always loved when you could see clouds at night. It feels like something no one else gets to witness. With them, however, you lose sight of the bear. The snow is accumulating. Large swaths of white lay all around you. You think about falling backwards and making a snow angel, but your toes feel like blocks of ice. A dagger of cold at your temples dares you to keep going. You don't want to lose your way, and you're a scientist and know that hypothermia is real, even outside of the tundra. Even in the wilds of suburban Wisconsin, you're at risk. Especially, perhaps.

You turn around and go back.

You wish you had told them all that there were no polar bears in Antarctica.

Just short of slipping back into the side door, you observe what's happening in the house. The bodies collected inside look like a multi-headed monster. A medusa of sorts.

You imagine yourself a modern-day Perseus and instead go knock on Ms. Horowitz's door.

Broken Keys

It wasn't long into their relationship that her "I" key stopped working. She started typing things like: "want to have sex" and "love beer & cheese." He took from these what he could and thought how lucky am I? I found someone who gives and gives and gives. Selfishness is not a trait he likes.

They wrote about their frustrations with jobs, friends, parents. He asked about her hair. Had she ever cut it? She asked about his roommate. Favorite meals. Her: takeout Thai. Him: homemade gnocchi. *It's so easy, anyone can do it.* She mentioned she had a window herb garden but didn't like to cook. He scoffed, but he didn't tell her he thought this was ridiculous. He talked about his recent case; he was an attorney. He began to type "tho" instead of "though" and "U" instead of "you," as if the effort for him to acknowledge who he was addressing was too much.

Like a piano with dead keys, it was beautiful until it wasn't. She saw the problem, of course, acknowledged it within herself, but didn't want to say anything. She couldn't afford a new computer and didn't see how she could replace the keyboard alone. All her letters, her words, slowly lost their meaning. "M" and "E" were the next to go. And soon he read her missives as that of a passive woman. In theory he didn't like it, but in reality, as he stared into his screen his own face vaguely reflected back at him, he thought that it was, in fact, the way it should be.

She typed and typed, late at night, at work, on the train to and from work, and she wasn't being any more understood, no matter how much effort she put into explanations. Her friends said *ditch him* and *swipe left babe*, though that wasn't the kind of app she'd found him on. He responded between the hours of nine and eleven at night.

Eventually, he wrote, *we are going to meet IRL.*

She typed, *ok!* Deleted it.

He saw three bubbles.

She typed, *what do you want to do?* Delete.

The bubbles disappeared.

She listened to the hiss of the heater in her little apartment, something she associated with both warmth and danger. She had learned how to avoid the radiator during the winter, one burn too many had left a scar on her forearm that still throbbed.

He typed, *Girl please.*

Girl? she thought.

What was all this for then?

She typed an angry mash of letters. *Tnwfuwfnwfrf!* Delete.

The bubbles reappeared. Disappeared again.

He typed, *did I do something to offend you?* and *don't say you're that kind of woman.*

That knd? She cursed her lack of an "I." She dragged her cursor to the *Log Out* icon. Hovered there. Clicked on *My Account* instead, clicked and clicked and clicked until she finally found, hidden amidst a throng of text, *Cancel My Account.*

A pop-up box: *Are you sure?*

Candy Necklace

When my mother left us, she gave me a candy necklace to remember her by. Surely, she knew it was meant to be eaten. Surely, she knew it would eventually just be a string hanging limply around my neck, damp and discolored white. Surely, she knew it was a poor replacement for a mother.

It's been a long time coming, she said. I was fifteen. What was a long time? Had it been coming since I was born? Since I was six and she threw me a My Little Pony themed birthday party, and my dad dressed up as Apple Jack? Maybe since the previous summer, when the three of us drove down that California highway along the ocean in a rented convertible, our hair whipping around our faces, my mom and dad singing – screaming really – to *The O'Jays*, into the bombarding wind?

As my mother loaded up her suitcases, duffel bags, paper bags, and that one vintage table lamp into the car, my father sat in his chair and flicked through the channels. There was nothing on, but he was someone who watched The Weather Channel for hours at a time. He loved Jim Cantore. He got excited when there was a big storm, somewhere else. He talked about La Niña like they were friends, and he could look at a meteorological map, put the TV on mute, and make predictions that almost always came true.

So it's strange he didn't see this coming.

This time, however, he only stopped momentarily on The Weather Channel. Stephanie Abrams was reporting on a flood in Tennessee. That was far from where we were. He had a crush on Stephanie; he had readily admitted it to us all. It became a family joke. Was it funny to my mom? I had no idea. This time, however, when the camera pushed in for a close-up of Stephanie's face, my father flipped the channel and settled on an infomercial about a counter-top oven that could rotisserie your chicken.

He dismantled their queen bed within days. I watched him heaving with that unwieldy thing, that emblem of their marriage, and dragging the mattress to the end of our driveway. He left it leaning against a streetlamp and started sleeping on the couch.

One week later, the packages began to arrive. I recognized the rotisserie oven. Later, sheets for beds in sizes we no longer had showed up. Buckets of dehydrated emergency food. Bulk mini bars of my mother's favorite chocolate.

Within a week, the mattress slid down and lay on the side of the road. It snowed and a light dusting covered it for exactly three hours. I watched. I kept track. A crow picked at it, looking for worms. A street cat took to kneading the tufted material. The garbage truck refused to collect it.

"Stephanie would never do this," my father said, head in his hands. I slid a glass of orange juice in front of him. "Oh, I can't," he said. "My reflux."

"That's mom," I said. "You don't have acid reflux."

"Oh," he said, and took the glass and downed it in two gulps.

He went into the living room where the shipping boxes had piled up. I followed. The items he'd purchased littered the room: dish towels, mixing bowls, fake jewelry, dolls from around the world, Christmas decorations, LED candles, twenty boxes of Zantac, throw pillows, vases, several sets of sheets, compilation CDs, two knife sets, a wooden chessboard.

He opened one of the sheet sets, in a color the package described as aubergine. He shook them out, grabbed the fitted sheet, and tucked his feet into the elastic. He then stretched it out and pulled the other side up over his head. He lay there, still. I watched his breathing under it and then left him there like a purple mummy.

Up in my room, was the candy necklace. I put it on. It was tight, meant for a younger child. I stretched it out, straining the string, but couldn't quite get the candy to meet my mouth. I let go; it snapped my neck – harder than I'd have expected. I pulled it off, let it drop on the floor, and left it.

Later, during a dinner of frozen pizza, my father stopped midbite. "What's wrong with your neck?"

"Oh, nothing. I don't know," I said, and excused myself from the table.

In the bathroom, I studied myself in the mirror. Caterpillar eyebrows and acne. Bright green eyes everyone complimented, just like my mother's. The necklace had left a mark, a faint red circle around my neck. I thought of that ghost story about the girl with the ribbon around her neck, where it was the ribbon holding her head on the whole time.

I went back to grab the necklace, intending to throw it out. It was a stupid consolation prize for losing a parent.

I wound the necklace around my fingers like cat's cradle. I was going to bury it deep in the trash. Back in the kitchen, I found the small television we kept in there was already on, my father clutching the remote. I pulled and yanked at the necklace.

As I wound it tighter, weaving it in and out of my fingers, a piece of the candy snapped off and ricocheted off my father's temple.

I laughed, but he gave no indication that anything had happened.

"Dad, hello. Hi." I waved my hands in front of his face. He blinked a few times. "Dad." I snatched the remote away from him. "I'm here, you know."

"I know," he was trying to look around me. "I asked you about the neck thing."

"What happened to The Weather Channel?"

"What do you mean?"

"You know."

"I'm just watching something else."

It was the Home Shopping Network and they were selling a sueded folder to display collected state quarters.

"Seriously?" I said. "You don't need that."

I snatched the remote from him and switched the TV off. I threw the thing, and it glanced off a counter; the batteries flew out and clattered on the linoleum.

My father glared at me. "You happy?"

"Me? Of course, I'm not happy," I said. "Are you?"

He stared back.

"What if we called her?" I said.

"What if we didn't?" he said and reached for the necklace. "Give it here." I did. He took my arm, holding it out straight and folded my palm in his. I could feel his lifeline and love line and all the lines that made a life. He wrapped the candy necklace around my wrist. Once, twice. "There," he said.

It fit comfortably, not too tight.

I nibbled on a little, yellow, round candy bead. It was sweeter than I'd remembered. I had forgotten. When I was in fifth grade, I got into trouble for eating a candy necklace in class. I was sent to the principal, which felt like an extraordinary punishment for something so small. It garnered a call to my mother. It's when I first learned the word "insubordinate."

Two months later, at my elementary school graduation, as every kid had passed my mother's seat, on the way to the stage, she handed a candy necklace to each of them.

That night, in a home without my mother, the necklace still tied around my wrist, I was startled awake by the sound of a closing door. I allowed my heart to settle and then got up. In the living room, my father was not on the couch. The light from under the microwave illuminated the kitchen. My mother used to do that, and my dad always argued that it was a waste. He wasn't in there either. I looked in the den. Faint beams of light came in through the slats of the blinds, and I could see that while his ghostly indentation was in the lounge chair, his body was not.

I opened the blinds and saw there, under the streetlamp, on the mattress, was my father. He had made the bed: the purple sheets, the pillowcases. He had brought two pillows out and his head rested on one of them. The other was puffed beside him and waiting.

I slipped on some shoes and a jacket and stepped outside. My breath caught in the chill. It was so quiet. I walked to the end of the driveway, certain I'd wake him up, but he didn't stir.

He was curled on his side, with the sheet pulled high and his fists curled under his chin. He snored. Not too far away, a coyote called. Raccoons twittered. A gust of warm air rifled through my hair, caressing my cheek. The season was changing, winter turning to spring.

I crawled in next to my father, back-to-back, feeling the rigid line of his spine. It was freezing, nothing a thin cotton sheet could help. But I felt the heat releasing from his body.

This could be home, I thought, if we wanted it to be.

May His Memory Be a Blessing

The way the dishwasher sounds at night. The way the light from the microwave illuminates the room just enough as if sharing a secret only for me. The way the papers on the fridge are eight-years deep. The way I can't tell if it's the streetlight outside or the moon streaming in. The way the book is laid out, mid-page, belly to the table. The spine creased forever. The way there are three pieces of popcorn left in the bowl. The way I think I can almost hear the hollow deep sounds of klezmer from the radio, even though the dial is dark. The way I look out the window and the frost on the ground emits steam. The way I look up and down the street and see no one. The way I look again and see a coyote trotting across our urban street like it belongs to him. It does.

I wander to the back of the house and look out the office window. The way these padded wool socks feel on my feet. The way I have to manually pull up the blinds, because you never got around to fixing them. Outside the plastic kiddie pool is filled with dirty rainwater from autumn, from before. The way two leaves spin around each other in a dance that they're choreographing with the wind.

The way the shrouds are still on the mirrors. The way your laptop is still open, screen black. The way the pen cap isn't on. The way those three coffee drips on the floor still lead to the stairs.

The way the other pillow still holds a ghostly indentation of your head. The way I sleep only on my half, even now, four months later. The way I still put the pillow over my head, so I don't hear your snoring. The way I don't sleep. The way the bar of soap has a tendril of your long hair clinging to the underside. The way your towel has grown mildewy on its hook. The way a smattering of tiny beard hairs confetti the sink and counter.

The way the grocery list says: ketchup, lox, seltzer, dish soap, Nilla Wafers, and something to go with cheese. The way you used ellipses. The way I go to the store with this list and wander the aisles for two hours wondering what was meant to follow those three dots. What did you want? The way I get back in the car and douse my hands in sanitizer. The way it burns the paper cuts on my fingers. The way I still use a collection of old postage stamps instead of the sticker ones. The floral way those stamps taste, the sticky residue on my fingertips. The way my hand aches after thanking everyone for their kindness during this time.

The way your khaki pants are pooled on the floor, as if you just stepped out of them. The way the mug sits on the bedside table, a muddy circle of dried out, old coffee at the bottom. The way your electric bike is parked in the garage, your helmet dangling. The way I will charge your bike's battery to ensure it has full power.

The way we have that special bank account for that one big trip to Europe. The way your name is still listed, the font is meant to be impersonal, but isn't. The way we chose not to go paperless for those statements, and they keep coming.

The way the sun goes up and the way the sun goes down, and the way I wake and the way I go to bed reminds me of you.

The Predatory Animal Ball

The Predatory Animal Ball was an exclusive affair, and a lowly field mouse would never have intentionally received an invitation. On heavy cardstock, like an old-fashioned scientific illustration, intricate sketches of animals snarled back at her. The scientific names of these members of the animal kingdom in cursive. The Latin made it all the more intimidating. The predators were not drawn to scale.

The mouse prepared some tea. She poured the warm liquid into a ceramic cup, which had come as a set. She now used just the one, the other dusty in the cabinet. It was the owl that had left her partner flayed, half-eaten, barely recognizable, but for his tail that forked at the tip. She found his body on a haystack in the barn. She hadn't been back inside since. They had bonded over their tails. Hers had been severed in an accident when she was young.

The next season, grieving season, she went out only for food. Her agony was a tumor that grew exponentially. She writhed in pain, though not physical, it hurt just as much. After several months, she befriended her own reflection, talked to the Window-Mouse, and finally reached out to touch her, only to feel the cold of glass in winter. She stopped talking to the Window-Mouse, stopped reaching out, and curled deeper into despair.

The invitation to the Ball was the first of any kind that she had received since her beloved's death, and it was as if she'd been waiting to be invited back to life.

The evening of the Ball, the mouse ran her shaky paws up and down her tail, which had gone dingy with neglect. Looking at her reflection in the window, she marveled at how the Window-Mouse looked so confident. The Window-Mouse looked away.

Outside the Ball, she watched from the base of a willow tree, its weeping branches the perfect cover. A sad mouse under a sad tree. The predators pranced, stomped, and slithered up the grand staircase and she marveled at the pageantry. But there were creatures obviously missing. The small, the vermin, the delicate.

The door was about to close after the last animal – a massive and maned lion. The mouse nibbled at her nails. What happened when you went to a party not meant for you?

She scrambled in.

But she had not thought this far ahead and found herself under the sudden scrutiny of hundreds of eyes. Wolf, tiger, snake. Hawk, grizzly, alligator. The owl was the only creature seemingly unconcerned with her presence.

Look at me. See me, the mouse thought. A low growl issued from somewhere on her right. A hiss of a snake's rattle. The wet licking of chops.

This was a mistake, and her partner would never have allowed this foolishness, this interloping with death.

The mouse took one step back and the predators took two forward. She scurried along the edge of the wall feeling the hot breath of those that followed. Ahead, one wall met another, a corner. No outlet. And yet she still ran.

Then, with a whoosh, the mouse felt a clutch of talons at her midsection. A tightening and then up, up, up. It was the owl. This is it, she thought. Kill me and be done with it. Her eyes were cinched tight, but her ears were wide open, as they took in the howls and growls and the murmuring of a party interrupted. Then she felt the smack of cool night air as they left the building.

She went limp as they began the descent, her body a loose configuration of what it should be. Peeking, she saw a field quickly approaching. The grass lit by the moon, it looked like salvation. A foot above the ground, the owl released. She hit the ground and tumbled feet over tail.

When she stopped moving, she stared up at the hovering owl, feeling like he was waiting for her to say something. "Why?" she asked in a quavering voice.

The owl mumbled something about not being hungry, stretched its talons, and flew off into the night.

The Thick Green Ribbon

The Ghost Tree Trail was meant to be an out and back. Marked as difficult and lightly trafficked. Nine miles with a four-thousand-foot elevation gain.

Lynn and Andy stabbed their hiking sticks into the muck and trudged through the switchbacks, sweat collecting under their base layers.

To their right, vertiginous drops. To their left, old-growth forest. Dense tree canopy broke the sun into shards and nurse logs hosted new generations of flora. Hundred-year-old firs and cedars, vine maples, all manner of ferns, huckleberries. Blankets of moss enveloped everything. In the air, loamy evergreen with wafts of decay.

At semi-regular intervals came the baritone call of a great horned owl, beautiful, but unsettling in the middle of the day.

"I gotta pee," Lynn said, and stepped off trail. Her feet sank in the underbrush. From her backpack she procured a fold of tissue, pulled her pants down, and crouched. She watched Andy approach a mushroom colony on a log.

"Think these are chanterelles?"

"No."

He started scraping. "Think there are more?"

"We're not foragers," Lynn said. He dropped them.

After a while, the warmth of her urine flowed, as she held her pants out of the way. She wiped, tossed the tissue aside, and returned to the path. Relieved, she smiled. "Let's go!"

"Leave no trace," Andy said.

"It's biodegradable." The wad of tissue hung between the branches like a tiny hammock.

After the next switchback, they came across a broad section of cut trees: two-foot stumps surrounded by splinters. Beside them, scrawny evergreen saplings: new growth. A sign from a paper company told them they were committed to nature, committed to maintaining the landscape, and so they planted a tree for every one they hacked down.

A sudden susurration of leaves on the nearby trees, like prayer. Like a graveyard.

"I think it's called a harvest unit," Andy said.

"That's depressing."

Two miles later, they reached the top. Loosening their jackets, they high fived each other and looked out at the view. A clearing of thousands, millions, of evergreens tightly packed and sentinel. Verdant breathing hills in every direction.

"It feels so good to get outside!" Andy shouted, holding up his sticks in triumph.

On a bench anchored to a slab of concrete, Lynn sat atop a carved *JC luvs FR*. Andy sat on a local record shop sticker. They ate sandwiches and nuts and took generous swigs of water.

After a while, they tightened up their boot laces and re-shouldered their packs.

"Shall we?" Andy said, reaching around to stuff his trash into a side pocket.

In his wake, crumbs, napkin shreds, and eventually the sandwich bag came loose and flew off.

After the first switchback, Lynn almost walked into a towering Sitka spruce in the middle of the trail. "I don't remember this tree," she said.

"You really remember them all?"

Lynn tried to sidestep it but tripped on a root.

"You okay?" Andy said, coming up behind her.

"Yeah, I'm good."

"My turn," Andy said, going off to pee. Lynn picked at some tree bark – pick, pick, pick – eventually loosening some. She fingered the roughness, noticed red underneath, almost like blood. She picked some more, debris raining down onto her boots.

"Check this out," Lynn called. They'd seen it before, but the light was different now and the color almost unnatural. Lynn wondered aloud what all these trees would look like naked.

"Furniture," Andy said. "They'd look like our furniture."

They laughed and continued on the trail.

"Should be coming to the crossroads," Andy said.

They walked and walked.

"Should be right here." Andy looked back.

Lynn pulled out a map and opened the unwieldy thing. She turned to orient herself, flipped the map, traced her finger along a line.

"We passed it."

"We didn't," Andy said, and when they turned back around, they were faced with a wall of trees, trunks wider than oil truck tankers, tall as multi-storied buildings. A western red cedar with its swooped branches was front and center, drooping western hemlocks beside it like guards. The trail heading back down was gone.

"These were not here," Lynn said. "What the hell is going on?"

"No idea."

"Are we at altitude? That can affect your senses."

"Barely."

Lynn approached the trees. They all had a ribbon of moss around their width, about two feet up. She ran her finger along the velvety line.

"Okay," she said. "Let's turn around."

"That's not the way back."

"Well," Lynn motioned to the tree wall, "We can't go this way."

They retraced their steps, looking for the crossroads they thought they'd missed. In no time, the tree canopy grew denser. The forest, darker. A rustling in the foliage.

Lynn moved closer to Andy and pulled out her headlamp. "It's not *that* dark," he said.

Minutes later, he pulled out his own.

They didn't find the crossroads and had no choice, but to walk deeper and higher into the forest knowing it was not the way out. The flora pulled in tight, narrowing the trail, until they were forced to stop. The trail ran out. Nowhere left to go. In a small clearing surrounded by a near perfect circle of trees, they dropped their packs.

Lynn blew her emergency whistle. Andy kept consulting the map, as if some new trail would appear and save them. They ate their emergency food rations, drank their water, and eventually slid their tired bodies down in exhaustion.

They soon stopped talking and only listened to the wind in the branches, the bouncy song of a chestnut-backed chickadee, the not-too-far-away roar of a cougar. A mama black bear and two cubs approached, sniffing. Raptors circled above the canopy.

The carpet of dead orange fir needles swept over the dead hikers, a time-lapse that took very little time. Dirt mounded over their fingers, then their hands, then their arms. The scrabbly hands of dried maple leaves scurried atop their torsos. Detritus filled their mouths, nostrils, eyes, and ears until they were absorbed into the forest floor leaving no trace of them at all.

A Greater Folly is Hard to Imagine*

The wallpaper had a trellis pattern meant to evoke the outside, tea on a Sunday, brunch with witty friends. The flowers – bountiful peonies pregnant in their beauty. She does not know these things intimately and so thinks they are mocking her.

Lush green ivy painted in vertical lines, floor to ceiling.

Inside, in the walls of the great house, the wooden doors are heavy as history. In one room, the young woman, deemed hysterical, given the prescription of solitude, spends her days with an embroidery hoop, herself, and the weed-like creeping of death.

Twice a week, she is permitted to venture out onto the grounds for chaperoned walks – promenades, they call them. When she steps out into the air, she breathes in the world. It is enough to fill her daydreams until the next outing.

Inside, were heavy damask curtains, an emerald velveteen settee, a four-poster bed – all very opulent. Be grateful, they say. She moves from one to the other to the other, all day and all night.

The ghosts of ancestors tickle her feet at night and dance in the corners of her vision. Her breathing is labored. They say she is insane. Her bleeding has stopped. They say she is a spinster. Her heart beats in a frenzy when she lies in bed talking with her dead sister.

She tries to slip out when the maids come, but she is cajoled and coddled back to bed.

She digs her fingernails into the walls, edging them into the slits. Pull and pull and tear at the wallpaper in long strips, like removing viscera from a body, stringy trompe l'oeil entrails. They are beautiful in that bloody, bodily way.

When they come in the morning, they remark on her raw fingers; her nails have become jagged claws. But her hair, the maid says, as she rakes through it with a silver comb, is still as lovely as ever, thick and braided, shiny like pennies. The young woman's fingers are taped together, and her hands are dressed until she only has two thick batons at the end of her arms.

The maids call in her father. "You have ruined the wallpaper," he says. "It is all in your head. We made this room beautiful for you. The doctor says nature can heal." He motions to the verdant wall coverings, the lush materials, the view out the window. "So, we brought it to you."

He leaves her writhing on her bed, where the wallpaper made caustic her blood, drowned her lungs, and killed her. Slowly, in her beautiful prison.

* *Attributed to a letter written in 1885 by William Morris in regard to his wallpaper containing arsenic. Many Victorian era wallpapers (as well as other items) contained Scheele's Green, a pigment that poisoned many.*

When She Opens Her Mouth to Sing

The brittle stars, in stop-motion, edge closer. My body is too wasted to move. The sea laps at my feet, and my cheek is pressed into the beach's wet sand, legs ensnarled in seaweed. The ghost of saltwater stings my nostrils, burns my throat.

I wanted to be a part of the choir. When Sean told me that they have no need for my ratty-haired slut self, I thought, I'll show him. I rarely saw my brother and no matter how often I showed him things, he always claimed a special kind of blindness. In this way, I was mostly invisible.

The auditions were at four and I'd have to leave work early. Stan would have none of it and besides, in addition to being my boss, he is my uncle. If I told him, he would tell my Ma and she said choirs are for young boys and fairies. I pictured myself as a little fairy, flitting about near the hearth, and out on the moors and around the forest edge. Instead, I worked at a soap shop and I was the daughter of a single mother who kept a tavern at the edge of the world. An edge that felt like a knife that sharpened when I walked along it, which I did often.

At work, I begged lady troubles, locked the bathroom door, and pulled myself through the window. Misty rain settled on the peninsula, which was the usual state of things. The tide was high, washing out the road in frothy increments. Drinkers headed out for happy hour and I was sure I was headed to my future.

A hollow sound like a voice filled the air. Tree branches danced to the disembodied song and white crests smashed the rocks in a pattern known only to itself. The voice, I told myself, was just the wind.

I rubbed my wrists where Sean had twisted and turned them night before. You really want it, don't ya, Sis? he said snatching my arm. When I threatened to yell, he twisted the skin until it burned and he said, like this? You like this? This is what all the boys say you like. I wanted to find out myself.

"Ma!" I called out.

"Ma's at work," he sneered.

I stretched toward the door and away from my brother's reach. He was ten years my senior, my half-brother really. He lived in the city and visited intermittently. He and his girlfriend Pam were rumored to marry within the year. Rumored they were two lovebirds and raucous Sean had finally settled down. I knew enough not to believe rumors.

He yanked and my body snapped back. "Like this?" he said, suddenly gentle, rubbing – caressing.

The foghorn blared, and in that moment, I freed myself, clamoring from the room, out of the house, and into the bisque-like air. Sean was fast on my heels, but I easily lost him a few meters into the forest.

At the base of a tree overlooking the ocean, I sang quietly at first, and when I was sure Sean was gone, louder. The flute sound of the wind on the cliffs picked up and it wasn't long before the deep music harmonized with me, and it was then that I knew it was the voice of the sirens. The alarm song. The danger is near song. The join us song.

And so, the next day I walked to the choir audition. The voices returned and guided me, warmed me, enabled me to move forward. I carefully stepped thorough the water along the quickly disappearing road, turning inland. The approach to the village was steep and I made my way down the hill cautiously.

When I arrived, the judges were gathering their papers, coats, and umbrellas, talking about the weather. One shook their head at me as I entered, pushing slick hair off my face.

It was ten minutes before the auditions were supposed to end. I had time. I shimmied off my jacket and let it clatter to the floor with its collection of enamel pins and zippers. While I want to say I took the stage, stashing it in my pocket, taking it with me to pull out any time I wanted, I trudged up the three steps and practically tiptoed to the microphone. I didn't take the stage; I didn't own it. I didn't even belong there.

"We've filled the spots," one said.

"But I still have time."

"Sorry," he said and squinted. "Isn't it your Ma that runs the tavern? Your Da was…"

"He was," I confirmed. The man looked down at his tasseled loafers. "He was," I said again, louder, into the mic.

"Go on then. Haven't got all day." They balanced on the edges of their seats, papers in hand, coats on, happy to imply I was keeping them from something important.

I clutched my wrist, which still burned. I adjusted the microphone. Someone coughed. In the not-so-far-distance, the foghorn bellowed.

Taking my cue, I opened my mouth, and out came an exhalation of relief and inhalation of something else. Something wild and pungent with regret. What was expunged from my gut and my throat were gallons of seawater. Out came sea urchins and silky fingered anemones, kelp in slippery strands, entire Atlantises spewed forward, a choir of their drowned singing, *remember me.*

I blacked out.

I awoke here on the beach, that tenuous space that isn't land and isn't sea, and is also both.

The brittle star stalks towards me, extending an arm. It says, "The sirens were ready for you."

I lift my face off the wet sand. Feel the suck that wants to pull me back. Wet whips of hair suction to my forehead and neck. The fog, I noticed, has dissipated. I pull myself up to sit.

"For now," it says, "you have all this," and the star waves its skinny arm around to the sky, to the sea.

Contained/Not Contained

The charred remains told Sarah it might be too late. The campfire smell should evoke the memories of sweet, burnt marshmallows and ghost stories, and Sarah thought that yes, what she was seeing were definitely ghost stories.

Her nostrils flared. There were no bird calls, just the distant thwomp of helicopters. Down the block, the sign for The Stonefruit Diner was lit, its neon a beacon beyond the tract of burned houses.

The fire was five percent contained. Flames licked the hillside. It was noon but looked like evening. The texts came and the warnings pinged. Sarah shut off the volume. The helicopters flew off and now there was just thick, pillowy silence. The hulking remains of five-year-old McMansions smoldered on either side of her. One mailbox was completely untouched. It was in the style of a tiny red barn, and she wondered if the HOA had approved of it. She assumed no and applauded this small token of protest.

A terrier crossed the street ahead of her.

"Hey, hey, come here," she said, and bent as she trotted toward it. It stopped and stared at her, cocked its head. Sarah reached out her arm to the small dog. She was close enough that she could read its name: Cookie. She tried to loop a finger around its red collar, but the dog yelped and jumped back, and ran off behind the remains of a home.

"Fuck," Sarah swore. "Fuck. Fuck." She contemplated following the dog, but after she took a few steps onto the lawn toward the house, a shutter fell off the second story window with a clatter and Sarah rushed back to the street. She continued toward the diner, clenching her jaw, keeping her ear out for the jangle of dog tags.

Her own house was in the neighboring and much older subdivision – mid-century flat houses with many bedrooms meant for big families. Her neighborhood still stood, but they expected this new flare to reach there by evening. This subdivision, named Plantation Lakes, had burned down the previous week. Evacuate, said the city. Evacuate, said the firefighters. Evacuate, said her neighbors. And they did.

After Sarah's father died, Sarah's mother started working at the diner. It was the neighborhood hangout, but Sarah refused to go when her mom was on. Dinner at home usually consisted of diner leftovers her mother had pilfered: dried-out turkey meat, limp pickles, over-steamed vegetables, plastic-packaged crackers. She never brought home strawberry milkshakes despite Sarah asking. The diner had jukeboxes on each table. Served Cokes with vanilla syrup. In high school, after softball games and on nights her mom stayed home, Sarah joined her team as they crowded into booths, and drank milkshakes and ate French fries until midnight. It was that kind of town. Racial covenants and casseroles. Neighborhood watch and block parties.

A space moonwalker, who was actually a firefighter, appeared from out of the gloom. "Ma'am, you shouldn't be here." A radio chirped at his hip and brought to her mind a russet-backed thrush. She told him so. He stared at her through smoke-ringed eyes. He brought his walkie-talkie to his mouth but didn't say anything.

"Go," he said.

She coughed. Once, twice.

"I'm just," she faltered. "The diner, ya know?"

"Diner?"

"I can treat you for a milkshake," she said. "You look like you could use a milkshake." She so wanted to bring someone to the diner with her.

His radio crackled. "Ma'am, the thing is," he took a deep sigh. "No one will save you." A breeze caught Sarah's cheek. It was hot.

"Ok. I'm headed home," Sarah said.

"This fire eats people," he said, and walked away. He said something indecipherable into his walkie talkie. Despite the warning, she kept walking toward the diner. On the current of air came a deeper odor, like day-old fry oil: burned plastics, bodies, lives.

Sarah married her high school boyfriend after graduating. He threw parties and coffee mugs. She just sat in one chair all night during the parties. Then he said he shouldn't have married a Jew, and so he moved into a house with the same floor plan in the same subdivision with the softball team's shortstop. *She'd found Jesus and Mark*, the shortstop had joked. The message had been relayed back to Sarah by a mutual friend.

Now Sarah took evening walks, listening, and watching for birds, and her ex waved in an over-friendly manner when she walked by his living room window. There was no other route to the nature preserve, so she waved back at him every time and hated herself a little more for it. She knew he still was abusive – she recognized the way the shortstop's shoulders and eyelids hung lower ever since. Sarah thought the bruises of loneliness might stick around longer, but they weren't as tender.

The light of the diner encouraged Sarah – fluorescent and nostalgic. The sun disintegrated. The smoke billowed. The glowing sign beckoned. She could go for a strawberry milkshake, a soothing trail down her parched throat.

Looking back, she couldn't see the house anymore, but her car sat in the driveway facing out, filled with the items that she had decided made her life. Her passport; her mother's wedding ring; her father's vinyl; her and Mark's ketubah in a fractured frame – something that her mother had insisted on, though Mark had scoffed at their tradition; and a first-edition framed Audubon

Society print of a bird pecking at a deer that read "Black Vulture or Carrion Crow" in elegant cursive.

Sarah tripped. Smoldering and somewhat spongey under her knees was a charcoal log. No, a cat. She quickly scrambled up, wiping the char onto her shirt. No, it wasn't a cat. It had been something. And now it was not.

The deep trilling call of a western screech owl called out. That wasn't right, it was the middle of the day. Were the trees the owls perched in gone? Sarah should go. She *would* go. A yank. She turned and ran toward her house. Her throat burned, her eyes abrasive against their lids. The ghosts along the side of the road nodded to her, as scorched pieces of houses fell. *This could be you*, the ghosts said. *Don't let this be you.*

Sarah felt contained, about five percent, but it was a start. The diner back there, all that could – should, stay.

Forever

You cultivate negativity like it's a fucking garden plant, I tell you. Not everyone can grow things, you say, calmly. Some people don't have green thumbs at all. They can't grow shit. You are addressing envelopes, stamping a return address, sticking on Forever Stamps in the corners.

Soon after I lost the baby, you began to collect lint from the dryer in a shoebox. Those balls of hair that looked like desiccated spiders. On the windowsill, you lined them up with seashells and pieces of sea glass we had collected from trips in the before times. But now, you're mailing the lint and hairballs to everyone on the spreadsheet entitled "wedding list B." You say they didn't send presents. I tell you we didn't end up moving onto list B and they weren't invited to the wedding; they didn't have to give us gifts.

Still.

You're angry, I say.

Should I not be?

I don't look at you and spill into the couch. Swipe through my social media feed. Death, destruction, violence, bigotry, death again. Murder sprees again. Plagues still. My thumb fatigues from brushing over all the corpses. I click over to another social media app. *Congrats!* I type on a post where a friend announces that she is pregnant. I add three balloons, one red heart, and a big yellow smile.

I can feel your eyes boring into me. It is sunny out, and the sun reflects in the blues and greens of the sea glass on the sill. I can see it in my peripheral vision. The color of lakes, the color of envy.

The sun hides behind a cloud, the sea glass grows opaque again. The light and the dark live so close together. You've re-arranged the shells and sea glass, and packaged up all the lint and all the hairballs. You are stuffing, sealing, stamping. These will be dispersed around the globe, these pieces of us.

I toss my phone aside and head upstairs. Step into the shower smelling the overripe, peach mildew smell. Pink splotches color the ceiling. I collect the hair I'd left there, clinging to the walls. Proof of life maybe. I bunch it up into a big brown lump, it's so light, my dead cells. Downstairs, I hand it over to you, and I grab a pen. Address the next envelope.

We are all beachcombing for something, you say.

Divinity and Life and War and Confusion

We baptize our children. It is the word of god and not torture, they say. We nod like we agree and watch them dunk the baby again. Sputtering, wailing, passed around. The infirm and the soon-to-be-dead try to get their history to spill onto the child, one tear or drop of spittle at a time. But they are parched. So I say, hang on a minute. I take their arms, frail and tender, and twist them in my hands. At first, they cry out in pain and then they understand I am wringing them out. To make water for the babies. And for the babies, they are willing to do anything. After, they hold their bruised arm like a baby itself. For a moment, in their minds, they think it is gurgling at them, and they smile and coo at the thing they are holding. But when a real infant is pushed into their arms, they don't think they remember how to hold it, though they'd had three. It's heavier than they thought it would be and chide themselves for thinking what they held just moments before could have been a real baby.

My mother would like this, they think. My father. They get this beatific look on their etched faces. They momentarily forget their parents are long dead. Someone says their name and they must pass on the infant.

My grandmother looks down at her empty arms, and startles that she is cradling nothing. "Want anything to eat?" I say.

"Do you remember that young man, what was his name?" she says. She thinks I'm one of her Army Nurse Corps friends from Hawaii, from the war.

"I don't –"

"With his skin, that skin was all loose, and he wasn't in his right mind and said he loved you, and you kissed him. Sue, you're a better woman."

She absently pets the baby's head in my brother's arms beside her. The child's eyes flutter and then close, falling asleep with the repetitive soothing motion.

I pinch my lips in. "I remember," I say. I want to tell her that it was her. It was her and not her friend. Not me. Not Sue. It was her the whole time.

She blinks quickly for a whole minute and then turns away. She is silent through it all, as if she doesn't want to wake the baby.

Acknowledgements

Many thanks to my friends and family who've provided me with support and love. A million thanks to my fellow writers who've inspired and encouraged me, given me feedback, and read and/or shared my work. To Tin House, Writing by Writers, and my many teachers: you've made me a better writer. To my extra special Twitter lit community: every day, I appreciate you. To Ruth Kambar, thank you for believing in me. To the journals and the editors who've published my writing, thank you for believing in me and making my work stronger. Thank you to Scott Driscoll, the University of Washington continuing education program, Hugo House, and Hedgebrook's VORTEXT. Thank you to Artist Trust and Pen Parentis for helping support my dream. To the women of my first writing group, thank you for setting my course. To my current writing group, Sarah Cannon, Allison Ellis, Candace Morris, Natalie Serriani, Natalie Singer, and Jen Warnick: how lucky I am to have you; I think we have another era in us.

For many and varied reasons, a special thank you to Joy Baglio, Maureen Henderson, Allie Mariano, Amy Blakemore, Kira Jane Buxton, Sharon Van Epps, Kathy Fish, Rebecca Makkai, Ramona Ausubel, Denne Michele Norris, Ronit Plank, Cameron Dezen Hammon, Michele Raphael, Cindy Lamothe, Brette Popper, Jo Umans, Erin Graham, Randi Menendez, Amy

Rogers, Regina Sather, Natalie Bicknell, Meredith Jensen, Janet Frishberg, Helen Fliss, Randy Englert, and Tim Fliss. To my daughter who reminds me that anything is possible with a little imagination.

To Eric, Genevieve, and the Okay Donkey Team: I'm so grateful for this opportunity. Thank you for your work. To you reading this book, thank you most of all.

"The Child Executioner" first appeared in *The Airgonaut*

"Towels" first appeared in *Atlas & Alice*

"Just the Air That They Breathe" first appeared in *Bird's Thumb*

"Sex Drive," "Watercolor Felon," and "Edward Scissorhands Takes Up Scrapbooking" first appeared in *Cease Cows*

"The Mourning Light" and "Evidence" first appeared in *Change Seven*

"Infidelity Love Suit" first appeared in *Cheap Pop*

"What Goes with Us" first appeared in *Cheat River Review*

"Mise en Place" first appeared in *Cleaver*

"The Last Time They Came. The First Time They Understood." first appeared in *Cotton Xenomorph*

"Swan Songs are Just Human Songs with Feathers" first appeared in *Fractured Lit*

"The Predatory Animal Ball" first appeared in *Fudoki Magazine*

"Broken Keys," "A Greater Folly is Hard to Imagine," and "When She Opens Her Mouth to Sing" first appeared in *Ghost Parachute*

"The Gargoyles Survey Their City" first appeared in *Gigantic Sequins*

"My Syllables" first appeared in *Hypertrophic Press*

"The Intimacy of Brushing Teeth" first appeared in *Lost Balloon*

"All Your Household Needs" first appeared in *Lumiere Review*

"May His Memory Be a Blessing" first appeared in *Macro(mic)*

"Mirror, ca. 1550 – 1350 B.C." first appeared in *Milk Candy Review*

"Degrees" first appeared in *Necessary Fiction*

"Trees Like a Way Out" first appeared in *Okay Donkey*

"Divinity and Life and War and Confusion" first appeared in *Parentheses Journal*

"The Great Bear" first appeared in *perhappened mag*

"The Inevitable Breaking of Limbs" first appeared in *Salome*

"Forever" first appeared in *Schuylkill Valley Journal*

"Contained/Not Contained" first appeared in *The South Seattle Emerald*

"Yolk" first appeared in *Syntax & Salt*

"Emily, Beside Herself" first appeared in *Thin Air*

"Pigeons" first appeared in *Threadcount*

"Grovel" first appeared in *Tiny Molecules*

"Dandelions" first appeared in *WhiskeyPaper*

"(It's not like Claire didn't bring it on herself.)" first appeared in *X-R-A-Y*

"Some Sort of Apology" first appeared in **82 Review*

About the Author

Jennifer Fliss received her B.A. from the University of Wisconsin and a certificate in Literary Fiction from the University of Washington. She's been nominated several times for both the Pushcart Prize and the Best of the Net and was selected for the 2019 Best Small Fictions anthology. Her stories and essays have appeared in print and online in places like *The Rumpus, PANK, The Washington Post, F(r)iction, The Kitchn,* and elsewhere. She was the 2018/2019 Pen Parentis Fellow, a recipient of a 2019 Artist Trust GAP award, and is currently working on her first (and second) novel.